CHRIST IS BUILDING HIS NATIVE CHURCH
STRATEGIES AND METHODS FOR PLANTING
INDIGENOUS CHURCHES

CENTRE FOR PENTECOSTAL THEOLOGY
NATIVE NORTH AMERICAN CONTEXTUAL
MOVEMENT SERIES

Consulting Editor
Corky Alexander

Christ Is Building His Native Church

Strategies and Methods for Planting Indigenous Churches

Joseph Jolly

Cherohala Press
Cleveland, Tennessee

Christ Is Building His Native Church
Strategies and Methods for Planting Indigenous Churches
Centre for Pentecostal Theology Native North American Contextual Movement Series

Published by Cherohala Press
900 Walker ST NE
Cleveland, TN 37311
USA
email: cptpress@pentecostaltheology.org
website: www.cptpress.com

Library of Congress Control Number:

ISBN: 978-1-935931-84-3

Copyright © 2019 Cherohala Press

All rights reserved. No part of this book may be reproduced or transmitted in any form or by any means, electronic or mechanical, including photocopying, recording, or by any information storage or retrieval system, without permission in writing from the publisher. For information, contact us at Chris Thomas, 900 Walker ST NE, Cleveland, TN 37311, or online at www.cptpress.com.

Available at special quantity discounts when purchased in bulk by bookstores, organizations, and special-interest groups.
For more information, please e-mail cptpress@pentecostaltheology.org.

Contents

Foreword ix
Acknowledgements xi

Chapter 1
Introduction 1

Chapter 2
The Indigenous Peoples in Canada 5

Chapter 3
Introduction of Christianity to the Indian People of Canada 29

Chapter 4
The Birth of the National Native Church 49

Chapter 5
The Indigenous Church Principles 67

Chapter 6
Developing a Native Theology 89

Chapter 7
Cross-Cultural Communication 111

Chapter 8
Strategy for Evangelism in Native Missions 133

Chapter 9
Conclusions 149

Appendix: The Beginning of NEFC 153
Bibliography 163
Index of Biblical References 168
Index of Authors 169

Foreword

The late Dr Richard Twiss founded Wiconi (a Native American contextual ministry) to 'create a better future' for Indigenous people. As the current Director of Wiconi, I serve our Lord Jesus Christ with the same focus. Dr Joseph Jolly's (Cree) focus in this book meshes exactly with my own reasons for being in ministry. I first read his dissertation when teaching a graduate class for NAIITS: An Indigenous Learning Community.[1] The dissertation was required reading for my class 'Missional Ecclesiology'. As I read the dissertation, I began to wonder why it had not yet been published. Not knowing Joseph Jolly personally at the time, I felt compelled to give him a call. During our conversation, we knew we were speaking the same language and had the same heart for the evangelization of Indigenous North Americans. I contacted my publisher, who graciously reviewed and then agreed to publish the dissertation. We believe this book will be a fitting addition to the growing body of literature about Native American/First Nations contextual ministry and assist those in ministry to more reach Indigenous people for Christ effectively.

Jolly's book title says it all: *Christ Is Building His Native Church: Strategies and Methods for Planting Indigenous Churches*. It reviews cross-cultural principles and examines the approaches and methodologies of planting Native churches with a focus on indigenization and contextualization. He shares much insight into the worldview of Native people, intending to provide a resource book for anyone interested in working among Indigenous people *anywhere* in the world.

Jolly highlights the differences that exist among three Native groups in Canada. He opens up a window and allows us to see a worldview shared by many North American tribes. He 'pulls no punches' as he shares the many mistakes and failures made by

---

[1] https://naiits.com/, accessed Apr.7, 2019.

Christian missionaries as they forced assimilation, colonialism, and paternalism upon Native people. I believe these ineffective styles of ministry are *still in common use* among many denominations involved in Native ministry.

Jolly then defines a biblical Indigenous church planting principle which focuses on the 'Three self-principles' that follow Paul's pattern for church planting. Jolly briefly touches on Native American/First Nations contextual ministry as authored and expanded by the Native theologians of NAIITS: An Indigenous Learning Community, of which I am a member, a published author, and an academic instructor. NAIITS is leading the way for others to see the need for and application of Indigenous self-theologizing. Jolly gives equal importance to cross-cultural communication principles to include language, culture, worldview, concrete relational thinking and 'contextualization' – a word many ministers taught in a previous style of ministry believe is associated with syncretism. Jolly and I both see contextualization as indispensable in reaching *any* culture. As Jolly shares his recommendations for Mission/Church relationships, he and I are both encouraged and believe we are in a *Kairos* time, a time God is opening for those courageous enough to enter.

In Acts 15.19, James says 'It is my judgment, therefore, that we should not make it difficult for the Gentiles who are turning to God' (NIV). In the past, indigenous people were forbidden to participate in and were dispossessed of their cultural and ethnic identities. Missionaries often believed that assimilation to western cultural ways was necessary for the salvation of their souls. Dr Jolly's words in this book will be used to open hearts and minds that have been misled for years by this mindset. His logical approach gives us 'marching orders' that can lead to a 'spiritual harvest' of Indigenous people.

> Dr Casey Church (Pokagon Band of Potawatomi)
> Director of Wiconi
> Professor for NAIITS: An Indigenous Learning Community.

Acknowledgements

I want first of all to say thank you to the Directors of Native Gospel Ministries of Canada for allowing me to pursue my studies. Then I want to thank the Cree School Board Post-Secondary Program for sponsoring me to complete my Doctor of Ministry Program.

I am grateful to many people who had a part in our ministry over the years. I want to give special thanks to Dr Dan Kelly and his wife Jan for taking the time to teach my wife and me the indigenous church principles while we were still in school at Briercrest Bible College. Through the years these mission principles have been instrumental in helping me to form a philosophy of ministry and to develop a strategy on how to reach our Native people with the gospel of Jesus Christ.

I also want to express my gratitude to Dr Tom Francis and his wife Helen for teaching us the indigenous principles from a Native perspective. Tom is the founder of the Native Evangelical Fellowship of Canada, Inc (NEFC) and was my predecessor when I became Executive Director. Before he stepped down from his position due to health reasons, Tom took the time to teach my wife and me these principles. In his wisdom he knew that our understanding of these principles would benefit the ministry of NEFC.

I would like to thank my advisor, Dr Daryl Climenhaga, for all his help and suggestions towards the completion of my dissertation project. I am indebted as well to Evelyn Turriff for proofreading and editing the final draft of the project paper. I appreciated very much her editorial criticism and helpful comments.

Finally, I want to thank my wife, Sheila, and our son, Joseph Seth. I want both of them to know how much I appreciated their understanding and support for me to complete all the requirements of my program.

1

INTRODUCTION

Church denominations and mission sending agencies have been working with the Indigenous Peoples of Canada for almost five centuries now. There have been some successful missionary endeavors in the past, but to a large extent Native ministries in Canada have failed to establish thriving indigenous churches. The slow process of indigenization may be attributed to the lack of interaction between the Native church and the non-Native mission sending agencies. Dialogue with each other is essential as they work toward the common goal of establishing healthy indigenous churches.

One of the problems in Native ministries today is a misunderstanding of the indigenous methods used in missions by both Natives and non-Natives. This misunderstanding stems mainly from a lack of teaching. People without formal missiological training tend to view indigenous church-planting approaches as too complex and based in human administrative methods. As a result they do not see the need to use these principles in developing a strategy of evangelism for the overall growth of the Native Church.

The purpose of this study is to review Native ministries in Canada, to examine their strengths and weaknesses as they attempt to establish true indigenous churches among the Native people of Canada. This study will show that good mission principles are scriptural, that they are essential for successful cross-cultural ministry, and that they lead to an indigenous church.

To resolve some misconceptions and establish a background of Native culture, the study begins with a brief historical review of the Indigenous Peoples of Canada, followed by stories of some early encounters with European settlers and Christianity. The intention is not to dwell on unfair treatment received by the Native people, but to present the uniqueness of Native cultures and the basis for some current problems.

From there, the research study will focus mainly on the goal of missions to establish indigenous churches. I will endeavor to show the strengths and weaknesses in Mission/Church relations when the indigenous methods are applied. In my study, I will explain the indigenous principles, their purpose, and where they first originated. I will explain the important role of the indigenous principles in the Native Church's strategy for evangelism.

Definitions of Terms

Native Ministries
Native ministries is a general expression that includes the overall missionary endeavor and evangelistic outreach to the Indigenous Peoples of Canada by local churches, denominations, mission agencies, and parachurch organizations.

Indigenous Church
Lindsell gives a good description of what constitutes an indigenous church. He writes,

> An indigenous church is one which has become Native to the land in which it has been planted. Its growth will belie its source of origin save for the characteristics of the church which should be common to all churches. A national church influenced by the soil in which it grows will reflect the land and people. It will have ties with the Universal Church but it will express itself in a way which will mark it off from all other churches. It will not be an appendage to something else or a carbon copy of other traditions, forms, and outward adornments. Above all it will have those three dominant characteris-

tics which mark it off as indigenous in that it will be self-governing, self-supporting, and self-propagating.¹

Mission Principles
Those who are called and sent into missionary service today can no longer afford to go out into the mission field without a proper understanding of how to minister effectively in a cross-cultural setting. During the last fifty years, there has been a dramatic change in the philosophy of world missions. In 1982, Edward C. Pentecost wrote, 'Missiology is becoming recognized as a science. It draws from the fields of anthropology, sociology, psychology, and communications, as well as from the experience of those who have pioneered in various missionary endeavors.'²

Out of the study of missiology certain mission principles have emerged. One dictionary defines the term *principle* as 'general truth or doctrine used as a basis of reasoning or a guide to action'.³ Charles Stanley writes,

> Principles are timeless, universal laws that empower people. Principles have infinite applications as varied as circumstances. They tend to be self-validating, self-evident, universal truths. When we start to recognize a correct principle, it becomes so familiar to us, it is almost like common sense.⁴

The primary purpose of applying the indigenous principles is simply to help in sharing the gospel more effectively. They are only tools that the Holy Spirit can use in building the Native Church. Strategies, methodologies, and philosophies of ministry must give preeminence to the Holy Spirit. Mission agencies emphasize the establishment of indigenous churches and hope to see a stronger and more aggressive church, a more rapid growth, a more effec-

---

[1] Harold Lindsell, *Missionary Principles and Practices* (Westwood, NJ: Fleming H. Revell, 1955), p. 258.
[2] Edward C. Pentecost, *Issues in Missiology* (Grand Rapids, MI: Baker Book House, 1982), p. 10.
[3] *The Compact English Dictionary* (1985), s.v. 'principle'.
[4] Charles Stanley, *The Wonderful Spirit Filled Life* (Nashville, TN: Thomas Nelson Publishers, 1992), p. 214.

tive presentation of the gospel, a wider outreach, and more wholesome relations between the missionaries and nationals.[5]

Ministry Experience

I am a Cree Indian, and I have been a born-again Christian since October 13, 1974. I went to Briercrest Bible College in 1976 for my theological training. In April 1980, after my wife and I graduated from Bible school, we went into full-time ministry with the Native Evangelical Fellowship of Canada, Inc (NEFC). I served thirteen years as Executive director for this Native Church body. In my work with the NEFC churches I was primarily involved in preaching and giving administrative leadership in establishing the Native Church in Canada. I had opportunity to interact with various mission agencies that were involved in Native ministries.

The ministry of NEFC promoted the indigenous principles with which I was working comfortably. However, I began to see that NEFC's philosophy of ministry with regard to the indigenous principles was often the cause of Mission/Church conflicts. Because these conflicts were based largely on misunderstandings, we had a lot of teaching to do on the subject of indigenous principles. I have always advocated indigenous principles in Native ministries and will continue to do so.

Today, I work as the General Director for Native Gospel Ministries of Canada, Inc (NGM), which was established as a ministry to reach, encourage, and equip Native peoples in Canada and the United States with the gospel of Jesus Christ. Following indigenous mission principles, NGM respects the languages, lifestyles, manners, customs, and various cultures of all Indigenous Peoples in its attempt to reach them for Jesus Christ. NGM's mandate is to promote missions and equip Native Christians to reach out within their communities and beyond with the gospel, that they may establish Native churches and ministries in all areas of Canada to the glory of God.

---

[5] Stanley T. Soltau, *Missions at the Crossroads* (Wheaton, IL: VanKempen Press, 1954), pp. 122-27.

2

THE INDIGENOUS PEOPLES IN CANADA

In the 1996 Census, over a million Canadians reported Indigenous ancestry.[1] With relatively high birth rates, the Indian population since the 1950s has been growing faster than the non-Indian population. This growth has nearly doubled over the last twenty-five years and has placed a continual strain on the demand for education, social services, and jobs.[2]

In Canada there is a widespread cultural renewal among Indigenous people. In reserves and urban centres there are numerous programs and workshops available that deal with cultural awareness and Indigenous issues. The primary purpose of these programs is to help Native people regain their cultural identity by teaching them more about their culture, language, traditional way of life, and spiritual values. The interest in Native culture and heritage has suddenly made it popular to be Native today.

There are many names applied to Native people, and this has caused much confusion and misunderstanding. To understand who the Indigenous people are, it is important to define some of these names. I personally take the same view as Edward J. Hedican in his preference for the word 'Indigenous'. He writes,

---

[1] Statistics Canada, 1996 Census, Indigenous Data, 13 January 1998; available from http://www.statcan.ca/Daily/English/980113/d980113.htm, p. 3.

[2] Edward J. Hedican, *Applied Anthropology in Canada: Understanding Indigenous Issues* (Toronto: University of Toronto Press, 1997), p. 12.

I have used the term *Indigenous* to refer to Native people in the widest sense of the word. The following definition is derived from that given in Section 35 of the Constitution Act of 1982 which states, 'In this act, "aboriginal peoples of Canada" include the Indian, Inuit, and Metis peoples of Canada.' My usage differs somewhat. I prefer to capitalize the term Indigenous even though a capital letter is not used in most instances because the word often appears as an adjective. I prefer the capitalized form out of deference to the wishes of the Indigenous peoples themselves, as a way of showing respect to their identity as distinct peoples.[3]

Along the same line Bradford W. Morse writes,

> This author is using the phrase 'Indigenous People' to encompass all people who trace their ancestors in these lands to time immemorial. This means that the term subsumes all Indians, whether registered under the Indian Act or not, the Metis, and all Inuit (also known as 'Eskimos').[4]

The term *Indian* was more widely used in the past than it is today. It is a misnomer that originates from Columbus' mistaken belief that his voyage had brought him by a new route to Asiatic India. Since Columbus' day, it has been applied to Native people of North America except the Eskimo (Inuit) in the far north.

The term *Native* is still widely used today, although it has been largely replaced by *Indigenous* as a general cover term. The term *Native* does not refer to a common or shared culture, but only to descent of Native ancestry before the arrival of Europeans. Today, often called 'The First Nations People', they are scattered virtually all across Canada. Each tribal group has its own unique culture, language, manners, and customs. Diamond Jennes writes,

> In Canada alone there existed over fifty tribes, each of which spoke a separate language or dialect and possessed its own peculiar manners and customs. There was no common designa-

---

[3] Hedican, *Applied Anthropology in Canada*, p. 5.
[4] Bradford W. Morse (ed.), *Indigenous Peoples and the Law* (Ottawa, ON: Carleton University Press, 1989), p. 1.

tion for the whole country, no single name for all its inhabitants. Is there any justification, then, other than a purely geographical one, for entitling all the aborigines 'Indians', with the implication that they belong to one common stock?[5]

Status and Non-status Indians

What is an Indian? This is a simple question that even an Indian person can have a difficult time answering. The reason for the confusion is that legal distinctions exist between 'status Indians' and 'non-status Indians'. Gerald Walsh gives a brief definition of who would be classified as a status Indian. However, we need to keep in mind that this was before the 1985 changes in the Indian Act. He writes,

> The Indian Act defines an Indian as a person who pursuant to this Act is registered as an Indian or is entitled to be registered as an Indian. If you are legally an Indian, you can live on reserves and are entitled to certain rights. However, a person may be a full-blooded Indian and yet may not be an Indian according to the law, in which case he does not have a right to membership on a reserve or any title to resources or reserve land.
>
> How, then, does one come to be defined as an Indian by this law? Normally, children of registered Indians are Indian. A woman, whether Indian or non-Indian, who marries a treaty or registered Indian automatically becomes a legal Indian.[6]

Hedican writes,

> In this context the term has a legal connotation because it specifies types of Indigenous people with special legal rights, as opposed to 'non-status' Indians, who lack the special rights conferred under the Indian Act. One can therefore interchange the terms registered, legal, and status to denote Indian people

---

[5] Diamond Jenness, *Indians of Canada* (Toronto: University of Toronto Press, 7th edn, 1977), p. 2.
[6] Gerald Walsh, *Indians in Transition* (Toronto: McClelland and Stewart, 1971), pp. 124-25.

who are a federal government responsibility. Because of the special rights that adhere to the term Indian in Canadian jurisprudence, those with special status under the Indian Act are not willing to dispense with it despite its negative connotation among some people. This is especially so for people belonging to the national organization representing 'status' Indians, the Assembly of First Nations (formerly called the National Indian Brotherhood), and its provincial affiliates.[7]

Duane Champagne makes some very important points regarding Indigenous Peoples:

> Although Indians, Metis, and Inuit are now collectively recognized as aboriginal peoples, their cultural, legal, and political differences remain very important as the Canadian state attempts to accommodate their respective demands. Indians in Canada have traditionally been subdivided into three groups: status, treaty, and non-status Indians. A status Indian is a person registered or entitled to be registered as an Indian for purposes of the Indian Act ... Treaty Indians are those persons who are registered members of, or can prove descent from, a band that signed a treaty. Most status Indians are treaty Indians, except those living in areas not covered by treaties ... Non-status Indians are those persons of Indian ancestry and cultural affiliation who have lost their right to be registered under the Indian Act. The most common reason for loss of status was marriage of a registered Indian woman to a non-Indian ... The situation for many non-status Indians changed in 1985, when the federal government amended the Indian Act with Bill C-31 to restore registered Indian status to those women and their children who had lost it through marriage. Indigenous women's groups welcomed this change. However, the response was not uniformly favorable; many Indian bands saw the bill as an unwarranted intrusion on their right to control band member-ship. The reinstatement process was largely

---

[7] Hedican, *Applied Anthropology in Canada*, pp. 5-6.

completed by 1991, adding approximately 92,000 Indians to the registry.[8]

In Canada there are many Indigenous Peoples who are classified as non-status Indians because they were not registered under the Indian Act. Bradford F. Morse explains how the registration system was implemented.

> The registration system was implemented by sending an Indian agent, appointed by the government, to the Indian nations to enumerate persons in order to develop treaty payment list or band lists. If people were away on hunting parties, out on their traplines, or off fishing, or if bands were in remote areas, then they simply were not registered under the Indian Act.
>
> Many Indians who were once registered, or who are the descendants of people who were registered, are no longer legally considered to be Indians under the Act. Over the years, thousands were persuaded by local Indian agents to become enfranchised under provisions in the Act.[9]

Many Native people gave up their Indian status in the early twenties, thirties, and forties because the Government put too many restrictions on them. For instance, until 1960, Indian people were not allowed to vote in federal elections, could not send their children to public schools, could not drink alcohol, or enjoy the provincially managed welfare programs. For several decades the only way to become a lawyer, doctor, or priest was to give up one's Indian status. Indian people were told that they had to become enfranchised and leave the reserves if they wanted to join the main stream of society and enjoy its advantages.

Some of the elected national Indian leaders today are lawyers and are very keen politicians when it comes to defending the Indigenous Peoples' rights. They know how to use the national media and the international political scene if the Canadian Government tries to evade its federal responsibility to the Native people.

---

[8] Duane Champagne, *Native America: Portrait of the Peoples* (Detroit, MI: Visible Ink Press, 1994), pp. 332-33.

[9] Morse, *Indigenous Peoples and the Law*, p. 1.

In the past and even today, the Government has pushed the equality for all Canadians which in the end would do away with Indian treaties, Indigenous rights, and Indian status. This has caused Indigenous leaders to stand up and defend their constitutional and inherent rights as the indigenous people of North America. In their minds, cultural genocide still exists.

Metis

The Metis are a mixed-race people. Some reside in Metis settlements, but most live with the general population. Alan D. McMillan writes,

> The Metis (from a French word meaning 'mixed') emerged as products of the fur trade, the offspring of European men and Native women ... Indeed, as a society born in Canada of two immigrant races (ignoring the Indians' lengthy tenure in North America), some Metis claim that they are the only truly indigenous Canadians.

> Historically the term 'Metis' referred particularly to those who were French-speaking and Catholic, while 'half-breed' more commonly was applied to English and Protestant individuals. The latter term with its derogatory connotations, has almost disappeared, with Metis assuming the more general use. Today it is applied to a diverse population, not all of whom can trace any ties to the nineteenth century New Nation on the Plains.[10]

Canada's Metis have often been called 'the forgotten people', and it was considered a major victory for them to be included in the 1982 Constitution as one of the three distinct groups of 'Indigenous Peoples'. The Metis now have their own national-level political organization, the Metis National Council, which broke away from the Native Council of Canada during the constitutional talks of 1982. Both Native organizations were represented at the First Ministers Conference on aboriginal rights. Hedican writes,

---

[10] Alan D. McMillan, *Native Peoples and Cultures of Canada* (Vancouver, BC: Douglas & McIntyre, 1988), p. 273.

The main reason for this rift was the feeling on the part of the Metis that the Native Council of Canada was dominated by non-status Indians whose main political goals revolved around a reinstatement of their Indian status. On the other hand, the goals of the Metis people have focused on issues relating to Metis identity and the assertion of Metis rights.[11]

Inuit

The Inuit of Canada live in the northern regions of Canada above the tree line, in small communities on the Mackenzie Delta, along the coasts of the Northwest Territories, on the shores of Hudson Bay, northern Labrador, northern Quebec, and scattered across the Arctic islands. The Inuit were formerly known as 'Eskimos', which comes from an Algonquian word meaning 'eaters of raw meat'. Today, they call themselves Inuit, which is the Inuktitut word for 'the people'. While they share a common language, they have a half-dozen dialects. McMillan writes,

> In 1939 the Supreme Court determined that the Inuit were included when the British North America Act made 'Indians' a federal responsibility. However, they are specifically excluded from the Indian Act, do not have reserves (although there are now Inuit lands under two land claims settlements), and are administered somewhat differently from Indians.[12]

Their national organization is the Inuit Tapirisat of Canada, which has been active in pressing for settlements of land claims and in the constitutional debate over aboriginal rights. McMillan writes,

> Unlike other Canadian Natives, the Inuit form a relatively homogeneous group and have remained the majority population throughout most of their traditional lands. A major goal has been the proposed split of the Northwest Territories to create

---

[11] Hedican, *Applied Anthropology in Canada*, p. 7.
[12] McMillan, *Native Peoples and Cultures of Canada*, p. 290.

an Inuit homeland called Nunavut, which could eventually aspire to status similar to that of a province.[13]

Total Native Population

Statistics for the total Native population of Canada have never been accurately compiled. Ovide Mercredi, former National Chief of the Assembly of First Nations, writes, 'At the time of contact, Indigenous peoples numbered approximately seventeen million in North America. Today our population here in Canada stands at approximately two million.'[14]

During the proceedings of a conference held September 30-October 3, 1990, Doris Ronnenberg, President of the Native Council of Canada, made an interesting point in regard to the Native population. She writes,

> The second perception which influences understanding of aboriginal self-government and self-determination is related to a political numbers game. Most of you in this room think of aboriginal people in Canada as a demographically insignificant minority, and you may have seen statistics that aboriginal people are only 2 percent of the Canadian population. That particular number is a reflection of the number of aboriginal people in Canada who are registered under the Indian Act – somewhere between five and six hundred thousand. A small number indeed next to twenty-five or twenty-six million other Canadians!
>
> By the same token, if we were to count the English and French populations in Canada only on the basis of those whose predecessors are registered as being born in France or England, how many 'status' French and English Canadians would we have? Even if we passed a European Bill C-31 and included those descended from French and English passenger lists to

---

[13] McMillan, *Native Peoples and Cultures of Canada*, pp. 290-91.
[14] Ovide Mercredi and Mary Ellen Turpel, *In the Rapids* (Toronto: Penguin Books Canada, 1993), pp. 18-19.

the 'New World', my guess is that the number would be surprisingly small.

How many people who call themselves French or English in Canada can actually name an ancestor who lived in England or France? Yet the right of those people to govern themselves in the context of an English or French culture is never questioned. In fact it is constitutionalized. When aboriginal people and their descendants propose they receive the same treatment for their cultural communities, they are asked to 'prove' that they are Indian, Inuit, or Metis. The fact is, most aboriginal people in Canada are not now and never will be registered under the Indian Act.

Several years ago, the federal Secretary of State commissioned a study on the demographic characteristics of Metis and Non-Status Indian peoples. In the context of his report in 1978, Christopher Taylor estimated that as many as 15 percent of the Canadian population has some aboriginal ancestry.

The point is that if the same criteria that is now applied consistently to English and French people were similarly and equitably applied to aboriginal people, we would comprise at least 15 percent of the population. But if sheer numbers are to determine who can and cannot govern themselves in the future, then we all better start learning Chinese.[15]

Since Bill C-31 was passed, many Indigenous people regained their Indian status. Statistics Canada today releases data on the Indigenous population of Canada from the 1996 Census:

> This report provides a profile of the 799,010 individuals who reported that they were North American Indian, Metis, or Inuit, about 3% of Canada's total population ... As reported in the Census, about two-thirds of the Indigenous population, or 554,000 people, were North American Indian, one-quarter or 210,000 were Metis, and one in 20, or 41,000 were Inuit. These numbers slightly exceed the total Indigenous population of

---

[15] Frank Cassidy (ed.), *Indigenous Self-Determination* (Lantzville, BC: Oolichan Books, 1991), pp. 37-38.

799,010 since a small number, about 6,400, reported that they considered themselves as members of more than one Indigenous group.[16]

In Canada there are over 2,240 Indian reserves. Most of these reserves are very small and many are not occupied at all. The largest Indian reserve in Canada is the Blood Reserve in southern Alberta covering about 535 square miles and having a population of 4,600.[17] There are over 630 First Nations communities in Canada.[18]

The Origin and Beginnings of First Nations People

Who are the American Indians? Have they always lived in North and South America? If not, where did they come from? These are some of the questions most often asked by people who want to know the origin of the ancestors of the Indians.

Anthropological Concepts

One theory is that long ago, there were no people at all in North or South America. But there were peoples in other parts of the world. About thirty thousand years ago, some wandering hunters from Asia entered what is now Alaska. They were the first people in North America. Others followed them.

> This small band of hunters was following a caribou herd eastward. They had no idea they were headed for a place no human had ever seen. They were moving from Asia into Alaska. They were the first people to reach the continent now called North America.
>
> All this took place about thirty thousand years ago. At that time, the world was in the cold, white grip of an Ice Age. A lot

---

[16] Statistics Canada, 1996 Census: Indigenous data, 13 January 1998, p. 1.
[17] Donald Purich, *Our Land* (Toronto: James Lorimer & Company, Publishers, 1986), p. 35.
[18] Assembly of First Nations, 'Description of the Assembly of First Nations' (Ottawa, 1999) http://www.afn.ca/afndesc.htm, p. 1.

of the ocean water had become huge mountains of ice called glaciers. These glaciers covered large areas of the earth. With so much water gone from it, the ocean was much lower than it is now.

The plain upon which the caribou hunters walked into North America was actually part of the sea-bottom. This 'land-bridge' nearly a thousand miles (1600 kilometers) wide connected Asia with Alaska. Today, it is under water. But until about ten thousand years ago, the land was often above water. And during many thousands of years, groups of people crossed into Alaska.

At times, the way out of Alaska was blocked by huge glaciers. But during warm periods, the ice barriers melted. Ways out of Alaska opened up. Groups of people moved south and east. By about twenty thousand years ago, there were people living in many parts of North America. By at least eight thousand years ago, people had found their way to the southern tip of South America.[19]

McMillan agrees that those whom we today call Native North Americans originated outside of the Americas.

Early writers, unwilling to see in North American Natives a people not recognized in the Bible, associated their origins with such historically known seafaring groups as the Egyptians and Phoenicians, or with the 'lost tribes' of Israel. An even wilder speculation was that the New World Natives were the descendants of those who fled the 'lost continent' of Atlantis before it sank into the ocean. Such ideas have not completely died out. However, several early writers recognized a physical similarity between New World Natives and Asiatic populations and assumed that an early migration of Asiatic hunters had taken place. Later, with the beginning of anthropological research, the Asiatic origin of New World Natives, across what is today the Bering Strait, became evident ...

---

[19] Robert O. Zeleny (exec. ed.), *The Indian Book* (Chicago, IL: World Book - Childcraft International, 1980), pp. 10-11.

The 'early man' advocates maintain that initial entry occurred at least 30,000 years ago, and possibly even earlier (a few speculate as early as 100,000 or more years ago). At the other end of the argument, the conservative view is that there is no convincing evidence for human presence in North America prior to about 12,000 years ago, when the distinctive projectile points of big game hunters known to archeologists as 'paleo-Indians' first appeared.[20]

McMillan makes an interesting point about an alternate way the Asiatic hunters could have crossed the Bering Strait.

Many archeologists reject the assumption that humans could have reached the New World only when Beringia was fully exposed. At its narrowest Bering Strait is only 90 kilometres wide today, and this width is broken by several islands. On a clear day land can always be seen. Crossing the Strait either on the winter ice or using some form of watercraft, would have been relatively simple. By comparison, Australia was first populated well over 30,000 years ago, despite being separated from Asia by a deep strait. The construction of watercraft would certainly have been within the technological abilities of people at that time.[21]

Some Native people will not accept the general agreement among anthropologists that human beings are not indigenous to the Americas. John W. Friesen writes,

Though the exact origins of Indigenous cultures may be unknown, what is certain is that First Nations have a long history on this continent and over time they have developed a distinct and discrete worldview. As Smith (1995) suggests, their firm belief that they originated on this land is for them a spiritual truth. They reject the Bering Strait theory on that same basis, and whether or not they are correct is not as important as the fact that their culture is founded on spiritual truths. Awareness

---

[20] McMillan, *Native Peoples and Cultures of Canada*, pp. 19-20.
[21] McMillan, *Native Peoples and Cultures of Canada*, p. 22.

of and appreciation for this orientation is essential if one is to gain an understanding of their value system and philosophy.[22]

Ovide Mercredi, former National Chief of the Assembly of First Nations, believes that the First Nations are indigenous to the land. He writes, 'We have always been here on this land we call Turtle Island, on our homelands given to us by the Creator, and we have a responsibility to care for and live in harmony with all of her creations'.[23]

As a Native Christian, I believe and accept the biblical account of the origin of humankind. According to the Bible, in the beginning of world history there was only one people and one family, the family of Adam. There was one language, one race, one ethnic people. But because of human wickedness, God destroyed every living thing from the face of the earth except for Noah's family. After the flood God blessed Noah and his three sons and said to them, 'Be fruitful and increase in number and fill the earth' (Gen. 9.1 NIV).

At the tower of Babel the Lord confused the language of the whole world. From there the Lord scattered them over the face of the whole earth (Gen. 11.9). Pentecost writes,

> The deluge came and went. Noah and his family replenished the earth with inhabitants, but the new generation of mankind was no different from the earlier generation. Sin was present. God did not choose to destroy the new generation. Rather He chose to offer a plan of redemption to all. The nature of that plan must be considered elsewhere as a study of theology. But here the relevant factor is that, dealing with mankind with a redemptive purpose rather than with immediate judgment, God chose to disperse mankind over all the earth and did so by initiating language change, cultural change, and family or ethnic change. At Babel (Genesis 11) we find the beginning of ethnolinguistic groups, dispersed into geographic, and thus

---

[22] John W. Friesen, *Rediscovering the First Nations of Canada* (Calgary: Detselig Enterprises, 1997), p. 21.
[23] Mercredi and Turpel, *In the Rapids*, p. 16.

physical situations, from which all ethnic, linguistic, tribal, and racial groups emerged.[24]

The Settling of the Continent

I personally favour the Bering Strait theory as a possibility in the settling of the continent by the first inhabitants. It takes both the anthropological and the biblical evidence into account. C. Roderick Wilson and Carl Urion write,

> All humans are related, forming one species. But some of us are more alike and some are less alike. It is in this perspective that we use the term 'Amerindian.' It suggests that in general the Indigenous inhabitants of North and South America are more like each other than they are like people deriving from elsewhere on the globe. This in turn implies that Amerindians have been here for a long time, long enough to become somewhat distinct from other peoples.
>
> The perspective of relatedness also suggests, however, that Amerindians are more like people from eastern Asia than anywhere else. This does not prove that the long-distant ancestors of Native peoples came here from Asia, but it does suggest it as a strong possibility.
>
> Even to a casual observer, Amerindians and people from eastern Asia share features that link them together and separate them from the rest of the world. People from both areas tend to have straight black hair, a lack of male-pattern baldness, and little facial or bodily hair; they have skin that tans easily, rarely have blue eyes, and have epicanthic eye folds. Less visible traits linking these peoples include the Inca bone (the occipital bone at the back of the skull is divided in two, the smaller, upper portion being referred to as the Inca bone, in commemoration of its first being noticed by archeologists working in Peru), and

---

[24] Pentecost, *Issues in Missiology*, p. 160.

the Mongolian spot, a purplish spot about the size of a dollar coin at the base of the spine.[25]

Different Indian Customs

The observance of their customs is an important part of the Native traditional way of life. In many cases their customs are sacred because they are strongly tied to spiritual values that have been passed on for many generations. Early in life, the Native people are enculturated about their customs and ritual ceremonies.

Respect for fellow human beings, especially the elderly people, is a custom that Native people teach their children. Native leaders recognize the role elders have in passing on their wisdom to the younger generation. Ovide Mercredi writes,

> I take counsel from Elders who are schooled in Cree and various First Nations traditions, as well as from those schooled in Christianity. We need to find wisdom in all places, to be open to learning about spirituality and how to live together. For me, the Cree ways are more important today than ever, for they will enable our children to have respect for who they are.[26]

Dancing is one of the customs that most Indian tribes like to follow at their ceremonials. There are different kinds of dances like the Sun Dance, Masked Dance, Give Away Dance, Prairie Chicken Dance, Horse Dance, and Elk Dance. At Indian Pow Wows there is competition for the best dancers.

Another custom among the Indians is to give and receive freely. Native people are generally very hospitable and friendly. They will usually help each other with no expectation of compensation.

Feasting is a popular custom that is observed during special occasions and events. On the Pacific coast, there exists a festival known as the Potlach. At this festival, the Indians give gifts to their friends. Their giving can become so extreme that the Canadian Government had to limit their giving.

---

[25] R. Bruce Morrison and C. Roderick Wilson, *Native Peoples: The Canadian Experience* (Toronto: McClelland & Stewart, 2nd edn, 1995), pp. 24-25.

[26] Mercredi and Turpel, *In the Rapids*, p. 26.

The Indians enjoyed being orators, so storytelling played an important role in their customs. With no books to read, they relied on the oral tradition of storytelling to preserve their stories and folklore. Around a campfire at night, an Indian orator would sway his audience with his words.

Traditional Beliefs

The Indians are a very religious people. Even before the white missionaries came, the Indians had their own religious system. There is a resurgence of traditional beliefs among the Native people today. Belief in one Supreme Being who is also called the Creator is universal among the First Nations People. Unlike some other religions, the Indian religion is monotheistic. John McLean, in his book *The Indians of Canada* (originally published in 1889) writes,

> The majority of Indian tribes believe in the existence of a Great Spirit, who may, or may not be the creator. He is not the same Supreme Being as that believed in by the white man, although the influences of Christianity oftentimes exert such a power over theological opinions of the Indians as to cause them to accept the Christians' God as the same.[27]

The Indians believed their God was eternal and had the attributes of omnipotence, omnipresence, and omniscience. Creation and providence are prominent doctrines in their traditional beliefs. Prayer and fasting also play an important role in their contact with the spirit world.

Another name for the Great Spirit is Great Manito. The Indians believe an inferior place is allotted to the existence of hell and a personal devil – *MATCI-MANITO* – Evil Manito. They believe in the existence of an Evil Manito who is similar to Christianity's devil.

Regarding sin, McLean writes,

---

[27] John McLean, *The Indians of Canada* (Toronto: Coles Publishing Company, facsimile edn, 1970), p. 108.

Though not taught explicitly, there is betokened in the recognition of sin the existence of a law, which belongs to the Supreme Being, and which, when broken constitutes sin, and man is punished by the infliction of disease for his disobedience. The soul of the red man cries out for forgiveness of sin, and this finds its highest expression in sacrifice. Sacrifices are made by some tribes to propitiate them, and their favour may be gained, and evil warded off.[28]

The Indians believed in the immortality of the soul. The Happy Hunting Ground was the white conception of the Indian afterworld. The Indians believed that all persons of all colours or beliefs who died unscalped and unstrangled went to a heavenly place. They also believed that one went just as he was, with the same passions, feelings, needs, and enmities. Since the Indian would meet enemies in this heavenly place, every warrior strove to reduce the number by scalping as many as possible in the world and by forcing their ghosts to live at ground level.

Vision quests were very important to the Plains Indians. When a boy reached puberty, his father or grandfather might send him out too fast. For several days the boy would weep, pray, and fast, concentrating on a desire to receive supernatural visitation. Torture was often exercised to quicken a visit. David G. Mandelbaum writes, 'While the boy slept, he might see a person coming toward him. It was the power that was to be his spirit helper.'[29]

As a Native Christian, I believe that Indians through their vision quests have contact with the spirit world. The stories I heard from my late mother clearly revealed that their guardian spirits could be used for good or evil. As in the past, hexing and putting curses on people through shamanistic powers is still quite prevalent in many Indian communities today. Former shaman or medicine men lose all their powers after turning to Christ which proves that demonic forces are deeply rooted in the quest for power in the Indian religion.

---

[28] McLean, *The Indians of Canada*, p. 109.
[29] David G. Mandelbaum, *The Plains Cree* (Winnipeg: Hignell Printing Limited, 1979), p. 159.

Their animistic background is probably the key factor why the Indian is so close to nature. Animism is the belief that natural objects are animated (made alive) by a soul or spirit. The belief is that within every object there is a spirit. The Indians believed the Creator has given all things equal right to live. Many tribes of the woodlands apologized to an animal after killing it, asking forgiveness of their friend.

The Indian religion claims to believe in one Supreme Being and uses religious terms similar to Christianity, but it does not accept the doctrine of the Trinity. Nor does it accept the gospel message of salvation only through the Lord Jesus Christ. As Christians we cannot compromise with a religion that will not accept these two important doctrines of Christianity.

The Native People's Contribution in Canadian History

The contribution of Native people in the founding of Canada as a nation cannot be overlooked. The Indians were often allies during times of war, and history shows that it was the Indians who taught the early settlers about survival in the harsh Canadian climate. The early settlers adopted many Indian foods such as pumpkin, squash, beans, and corn.

Indian persons today have many reasons to be proud about their ancestry if they are properly informed through the educational system. For example, history courses taught in elementary school need to give more credit to the Native people. Without the help of the Indians, the early explorers would have found their explorations very difficult. It was the Indians who showed the explorers the location of rivers, seas, and the great lakes. In the past, this was never emphasized in the classroom setting, and as a result many Native students were not aware of this.

Obstacles that Indigenous People Must Overcome

If we want to reach the Indigenous Peoples with the gospel, we must be sensitive to their social and political concerns. Before the white man came, the First Nations People were proud of their cultural heritage, but today they are considered as Canada's principal racial minority and often they are looked upon as outsiders and second-class citizens. Donald Purich writes, 'The image that many Canadians have of Native people is that they are lazy, shiftless, often drunk, always getting into trouble, and riding high on the government gravy train'.[30]

Indian people will tell you from personal experience that it is not that easy to live in today's mainstream white society. Prejudice, discrimination, inferior treatment, and stereo-typing are just some of the obstacles that Indians must overcome if they want to fit in. Based on these facts, it is not hard to figure out why so many Indian people struggle with a low self-image. Hedican writes,

> Federal statistics (Canada 1980; Corrigan 1991; Silverman and Nielsen 1992) provide a vivid picture of the massive obstacles that confront Indians today. For example, the average Native's income is but two-thirds of the national figure, and among Indians living on reserves, 60 percent are on welfare and another 30 percent receive their income from part-time jobs, short-term training programs, or unemployment insurance. In brief, the history of Canada's past policies towards Indigenous people has been largely a failure.[31]

Gary Quequish, a Saulteaux Indian from Weagamow Lake, Ontario, has worked over twenty years as a minister of the gospel among his own people. Besides his pastoral responsibilities, he has been quite involved in a counseling ministry. In his MA thesis on 'Effective Biblical Counseling Among Ojibway Peoples', he writes,

> The influence of Euro-Canadian culture has impacted northern communities in negative ways. The very fabric of their Indian culture has become disrupted. Parents are unable to relate to the 'new' cultural values and changes. Worse yet, many parents struggle with the pain of their heart. Many attempt to drown their sorrows in alcohol and drugs.

---

[30] Purich, *Our Land*, p. 10.
[31] Hedican, *Applied Anthropology in Canada*, p. 12.

Children are filled with shame because of treatment they receive from parents, ranging from abandonment to sexual molestation. Few parents know how to guide them through the difficult teenage years. This results in many turning to drugs, alcohol, sexual promiscuity, and solvent abuse. These vices run rampant in their communities. Many children and youth carry enormous pain, and despair, and are victimized beyond description.

Other changes are impacting the Ojibway Peoples in both positive and negative ways. Large corporate companies are moving north to rape the land of its resources, while providing badly needed employment for a few. Large hydro dams are built, destroying an entire way of life for numerous communities. Many fishing, hunting, and trapping lands are permanently flooded.

Modernization of many northern communities has brought with it great socio-cultural upheaval. The healthy traditional values are disrupted resulting in the fracture of community structure.[32]

Indigenous Self-Government

As a Native Christian I have personal convictions regarding Native self-government. We usually hear only the views of secular Indian leaders. In working with Native Christians across Canada, I have sensed that they, like me, fully support self-government.

Today in Native ministries, the goal of most missions is to establish strong indigenous churches. They do that by training Native Christians to be leaders of their own people. Indians reaching Indians is the quickest and most effective way to present the gospel to the Native people.

This principle of indigenous missions is somewhat identical to the principles being advocated in Indigenous self-government. Ownership and self-government are just two characteristics of an

---

[32] Gary Quequish, 'Effective Biblical Counseling Among Ojibway Peoples' (MA thesis, Briercrest Biblical Seminary, 1994), p. 41.

indigenous church. The way for Indigenous people to get back on their feet is to take responsibility for their own future. The same is true for Native ministries.

It is difficult to explain Indigenous self-government because the subject is so broad and controversial. However, as I understand Indigenous self-government, I fully support the idea. As a Native Christian leader I am encouraged when I see my own people take a greater responsibility in helping themselves. Indigenous self-government will help eliminate Native people's dependency on governments.

What do Indigenous people mean by self-government? Carol Goar's editorial in the *Toronto Star* is helpful.

> Native self-government includes control over their land and resources, the right to apply their own laws, protect Native languages, do their own policing, take over the education of their own children, develop their own health care system, set their own economic priorities, and administer their own social programs. And they want to be recognized as a distinct founding people.[33]

Another word used by Native leaders in talking about self-government is 'sovereignty'. This idea has been at the heart of Indian concerns for centuries. We want to exercise control over our lands and people. When the Canadian Government entered into treaties with the Indians, they proceeded on a nation-to-nation basis. What Native leaders want now is to have Native sovereignty recognized in the Constitution.

Indians argue that sovereignty is not that which comes to them by government decree but that which is 'a gift from the Creator'. Indians believe this has never been surrendered by any of our treaties. Mercredi writes,

> However, our right to govern ourselves does not come from European proclamations or treaties; they just recognized what we were doing already. The Proclamation of 1763 did not create aboriginal land rights – it acknowledges them as pre-

---

[33] Carol Goar, 'Why Ottawa's Plan Has Natives Angry', *The Toronto Star* (28 September 1991), p. D5.

existing. We believe, as we are told by our Elders, that our peoples were placed on this land by the Creator, with a responsibility to care for and live in harmony with all her Creation. By living this way, we cared for the Earth, for our brothers and sisters in the animal world and for each other. Fulfilling these responsibilities meant we governed ourselves, and lived a certain way. This is the source of our inherent right of self-government. It has a history that precedes the Charlottetown Accord by more than a millennium.[34]

Even though certain historical documents recognize the inherent rights of Indigenous peoples, federal and provincial governments have, throughout most of the twentieth century, refused to recognize Indian sovereignty. However, this is changing.

The Supreme Court's ruling in the Musqueim case (1985) has also persuaded the two levels of government to rethink their previous position. In this case, the Court recognized that Indian sovereignty and Indian rights are *independent and apart* from the Crown.[35]

The Native political leaders' persistent stand on Indigenous self-government has begun to pay off. The Canadian public is now more supportive of the Native people's cause for self-government. The federal and provincial governments are beginning to rethink their position. In fact, in August 1991, the Ontario government acknowledged the Native people's right to self-government. Frideres writes,

While there is some disagreement among Native groups on how to implement self-government, they agree that what they are seeking is a third order of government within Confederation. This would allow them to have direct control over areas such as culture, language, religion, and education, as well as administrative jurisdiction over Native land and resources. At the same time, the federal and provincial governments would

---

[34] Mercredi and Turpel, *In the Rapids*, p. 31.
[35] James S. Frideres, *Native Peoples in Canada: Contemporary Conflicts* (Scarborough, ON: Prentice Hall Canada, 3rd edn, 1988), p. 343.

retain those powers which would be exercised in the common interest of both Natives and Non-Natives.[36]

While I fully support Indigenous self-government, I do have two personal concerns. First, not all Native groups are interested in self-government now or feel they are capable of administering their affairs today. Much of the agitation for sovereignty comes from reserves who already have a sound economic base and proven leadership. Secondly, I am concerned that non-Natives assume that all Native peoples trust in the traditional beliefs associated with Indians. The majority of Native people in Canada embrace Christianity as their religion. Native Christians should speak out about their religious convictions to the media, helping them to understand the importance of Christian faith to many aboriginals.

Indigenous self-government is very similar to self-government in the Native church.[37] The main difference is that one deals with secular issues while the other focuses on spiritual matters. Traditional religious beliefs are closely tied to Indigenous self-government, as Christian beliefs are to the self-government in the church.

In their efforts for self-government, Indian leaders see a parallel between the government and the mission because both are comprised of mostly white people. Ethnocentricity by the dominant group has been one of the problems in striving for Indigenous self-government. Similarly, ethnocentrism by the early missionaries was a hindrance in planting indigenous churches.

History shows how the Canadian government and the early missions made mistakes in their policies and dealings with the Indigenous people. The aim of Indigenous self-government and self-government in the church is to correct the mistakes and negative impact that Western paternalism and policies of assimilation and colonialism had on Indigenous people. Indigenous self-government and self-government in the church both strive for autonomy and they share the same views and aspirations regarding self-government for their people. The principles of self-government,

---

[36] Frideres, *Native Peoples in Canada*, pp. 344-58.
[37] See the discussion of the principle of self-government in Chapter Four.

self-support, and self-propagation in church planting challenge paternalism and do not accept colonialism. These indigenous principles apply not only in planting independent churches but also in helping different nations to achieve their independence.

3

INTRODUCTION OF CHRISTIANITY TO THE INDIAN PEOPLE OF CANADA

The history of Christianity's early encounter with the Indian people of Canada clearly shows the success of Indian missions. Missiologists point out that the methods and means of evangelism employed by the early missionaries were ethnocentric but also that there was a great spiritual awakening among the Native people virtually all across Canada. Today, the majority of Native people name Christianity when asked their religious background. As John Webster Grant points out, Christianity is not a recent arrival but has been a factor in Indian life for almost four hundred years. Over many generations Indians have been making the sign of the cross, treasuring prayer books in their own tongues, singing hymns to Jesus, and performing various leadership functions within Christian communities.[1]

The Christian religion in Canada was established and maintained by Protestants and Roman Catholics in a dual culture. In personnel and financial support, they came originally from France, Great Britain, and the Thirteen Colonies. The ideas of Canadian Christianity largely reflected these outside influences, not only in matters of basic belief, but also in controversies over such subjects as church establishment and clergy reserves. From the period of

---

[1] John Webster Grant, *Moon of Wintertime* (Toronto: University of Toronto Press, 1984), p. 264.

origins (c.1600) to the present, five religious groups have comprised the greater part of the Christian community in Canada: Roman Catholics, Anglicans, Presbyterians, Methodists, and Baptists.[2]

Catholic Missions

The first recorded presentation of Christian teaching to Indians within the present boundaries of Canada took place at Gaspe on the twentieth of July 1534, when Jacques Cartier erected a cross and indicated as well as he could to visiting Iroquoians from Stadacona, now Quebec, that they should look to it for their redemption. In the following year his crew harangued the villagers of Stadacona on the folly of their beliefs and elicited in response what they interpreted as a mass request for baptism. On his departure, Cartier took several Indians, including the Chief Donnacona, to France, where at least three of them received baptism before their premature deaths.[3]

Samuel de Champlain (c.1570-1635), the virtual founder of New France, brought Franciscan *Recollets* from France, hoping they would Christianize the Indians. In 1625 the Jesuits joined the *Recollets* in Quebec and soon became the dominant element in mission work among the Indians, particularly in the Huron country south of Georgian Bay.[4]

The primary aim of the missionaries was to save Indian souls. Grant points out that the missionaries also saw themselves as agents of French civilization. During these early years, all missionaries conceived of France and the Roman Catholic Church as twin pillars of an indivisible structure. They rejoiced when Indians preferred French culture to their own, seeing in a taste for things French a significant step towards Christian faith. They planned their seminaries as agents of assimilation and sent a few of their brightest prospects to France for finishing.[5]

---

[2] D.C. Masters, 'Canada', in J.D. Douglas (ed.), *The New International Dictionary of the Christian Church* (Grand Rapids, MI: Zondervan, 1978), p. 186.
[3] Grant, *Moon of Wintertime*, p. 3.
[4] Masters, 'Canada', p. 186.
[5] Grant, *Moon of Wintertime*, p. 31.

Protestant Missions

Protestant churches entered Canada from both Britain and the British American colonies. They were largely supported by British missionary societies. The Anglicans drew support from pre-Loyalist New Englanders, United Empire loyalists, British garrisons and administrators, and immigrants from the British Isles. The Methodists consisted chiefly of British Wesleyans and American Episcopal Methodists. Presbyterianism, while derived from Britain and the United States, reflected the traditional breach between the Church of Scotland and the various Secession churches. The Baptist Church was pioneered in the Maritimes, in the Eastern Townships of Quebec, and in the Niagara Peninsula from the United States, but also derived support from the Scottish Highlands. The Lutheran Church in Canada kept pace with the immigration of German and Scandinavian peoples. The Lutherans established their first permanent congregation in Nova Scotia about 1750 and entered Upper Canada some twenty-five years later.[6]

Expansion of the churches continued in the late nineteenth century and resulted also in ecumenical movements of organized reunion and confederation. The Presbyterians in Canada were united in 1875, most of the Methodists in 1884, and the Anglican General Synod was formed in 1893. In 1925 the Methodist and Congregational churches and a large part of the Presbyterian Church united to form the United Church of Canada.[7]

Participation of the Canadian churches continued. Domestic missions among the North American Indians and Eskimos were chiefly maintained by the Roman Catholic, the Anglican, and the United churches.[8]

---

[6] Masters, 'Canada', p. 186.
[7] Masters, 'Canada', p. 186.
[8] Masters, 'Canada', p. 187.

Pattern of Missions

In dealing with the pattern of early Indian missions, Grant writes that the missionary on an Indian reserve was a person of considerable importance, exercising functions far beyond those of spiritual oversight. He mentions that in addition to assuming general responsibility for education and welfare, he or she was likely to be called upon to administer first aid, dispense drugs, and even perform surgery. There might also be occasional calls to adjudicate local disputes. A missionary who spoke an Indian language was a natural person to represent Indian desires to the authorities and to interpret government policies to the Indians. Some missionaries promoted the economic progress of their communities, managing stores, and establishing industries.[9]

According to Kelly, the man who most exemplified the attitudes and methods of early missionaries was William Duncan. Kelly mentions that the story of Duncan of Metlakatla has been well told in other writings but a few details are worth repeating.

> Duncan was trained at Highbury Missionary College of the CMS in London and while he was attending school, Captain Prevost of the British Navy requested that the Church Missionary Society supply a missionary for the North Pacific Coast of America. At the age of 26 Duncan arrived in Victoria aboard the naval warship Satellite ...
>
> Duncan moved to Fort Simpson in September of 1857 and began to study the language of the Tsimshean Indians. He did very little evangelistic work until he had some confidence in the language, which took about eight months. By 1861, he had gathered a small contingent of believers, but he determined that the Indians could not live a consistent Christian life in their Fort Simpson environment. He therefore decided to build a Christian community in which no pagan influence could flourish. In May of 1862, Duncan and fifty converts left Fort Simpson and moved fifteen miles to the site of the proposed Christian village. Shortly after, another 300 Indians moved to

---

[9] Grant, *Moon of Wintertime*, p. 173.

Metlakatla and within a very few years the town grew to be one of the largest communities on the north coast with a population of over 1,000.

Duncan did not limit himself to evangelism. He founded a sawmill, a store, and a salmon cannery. The Metlakatla Indians had a brass band, a choir, a fire department, and a ladies missionary circle. The church, which had been dubbed Duncan's 'Westminster Abbey', was built on the European model and seated 1,000 people. The missionary was the judge, jury, mayor, general manager, and pastor of the community.[10]

Another pattern of Indian missions was that all denominations sought to make room for Indian leadership within the mission church. Some of them offered openings as elders, church wardens, or class leaders; but for an Indian to rise higher in the ecclesiastical hierarchy was more difficult. In an Anglican community there was a good chance that the local missionary would be Indian or part-Indian, for in 1916 the Missionary Society of the Canadian Church reported seventy-five Native agents in its employ in Indian missions and ninety-two white. Roman Catholics made a point of having priests in charge of every mission, and practically all priests were white. The Presbyterians, who ran their Indian missions from Winnipeg, ordained a few Indians and others born here, and employed a fair number as school teachers. The Methodists, once pacesetters in making use of Native preachers, were reduced by the end of the nineteenth century to a few, mostly aging clergy. Protestants found Indians useful in reaching their people, but preferred whites as mediators of civilization. Such, at any rate, was the reasoning of the Methodist mission secretary, Alexander Sutherland. Whatever the denomination, Indian congregations had no voice in the selection of their missionaries. Whatever the denomination, moreover, even Indians who attained positions of local leadership had virtually no access to the centres of power of the agencies that controlled the missions.[11]

---

[10] Daniel P. Kelly, *Indigenous Church Principles* (Vernon, BC: Laurel Publications, 1977), pp. 77-78.

[11] Grant, *Moon of Wintertime*, p. 174.

Assimilation as Policy

The basic meaning of the word 'assimilate' is to make similar. A simple definition of assimilation is to absorb and incorporate as part of itself.

The early European explorers who came to North America were essentially motivated by greed. In their search for gold and glory they exploited the land and its natural resources. When they encountered the First Nations resident in the new land, their philosophy was to bring them into their economic system or, if that was not possible, take their gold and eliminate them.[12]

Initially, the French were interested in the New world as a source of wealth capable of financing wartime activities. It was hoped that the land would hold precious metals that would rival in worth those found in Spanish America. Throughout the sixteenth century, fishing and whaling were the major economic activities that attracted more and more Europeans to North America. It was only at the end of the sixteenth century that fur trade began to grow into an important economic activity.[13]

Friesen points out that the objective of the missionary movement that followed on the heels of the fur trade was corollary to economic pursuits, with a sense of mission to change the customs and lifestyle of the dwellers in the new world. This was to be accomplished through whatever means available, economic, religious, or ideological. It eventually became evident that one of the most viable means by which to fulfill this mission was through schooling – by educating young Natives in European ways, the future takeover of the country would be assured.[14]

Missionaries stated that their intentions were not primarily to achieve economic gain in the new world; they really came to 'Christianize, educate, and civilize' the Indian. Through their actions, it later became evident that they became, perhaps somewhat inadvertently, the principal agents of European assimilation.[15]

---

[12] Friesen, *Rediscovering the First Nations of Canada*, p. 204.
[13] Frideres, *Native Peoples in Canada Contemporary Conflicts*, p. 18.
[14] Friesen, *Rediscovering the First Nations of Canada*, p. 204.
[15] Friesen, *Rediscovering the First Nations of Canada*, p. 205.

The policy of assimilation was strengthened by a number of supporting policies, one of which was the spread of Christianity to the Indian population.

> In Canada the civilization of the Indian is made synonymous with his Christianization. Indian missions, in fact, enjoy government favour; the aboriginal religious and ceremonial practices are officially discouraged. Next to the attainment of the goal of self-support, the Indian's conversion from pagan belief to Christianity is the most important criterion for judging his fitness to assume an equal place in the white man's society.[16]

The church came to play a very important role in the education of Indians. In the early years, education was viewed, as it still is in many quarters, as an essential tool of assimilation. The responsibility for Indian education, however, was largely delegated by the government to the churches. In the long run this strategy was to prove unsatisfactory. Because the religious residential schools isolated Indians from other students, assimilation was impaired. Because their curricula served as much as a vehicle for Christianization as for secular, the secular education of Indians suffered in comparison to that received by non-Indians. Finally, the residential schools were a source of great disruption and antagonism within the Native communities and did little to enhance the value of education in the eyes of Native students.[17] By the 1960s, the traditional role of the church in Indian affairs was drawing to a close.

If there has been a central pillar to Canadian policy, it has been the goal of assimilation. While the terminology has varied among 'assimilation', 'integration', 'civilization', and 'moving into the mainstream', the policy has remained virtually unaltered; Indians were to be prepared for absorption into the broader Canadian society. It was expected that eventually Indians would shed their Native language, customs, and religious beliefs and become self-sufficient members of the modern Canadian society and labour

---

[16] J. Rick Ponting (ed.), *Arduous Journey: Canadian Indians and Decolonization* (Toronto: McClelland & Stewart, 1991), p. 27.

[17] Ponting (ed.), *Arduous Journey*, pp. 27-28.

force.¹⁸ The goal of assimilation raises the very sensitive issue of cultural genocide.

Despite the zeal with which assimilation was pursued, the policy largely failed. Due to the Indian's isolation on reserves, racial and linguistic distinctiveness, marginality to the labour force, and the gulf between Native and European cultural patterns, Indians proved to be a difficult group to assimilate. A large part of the responsibility for the failure of assimilation must be laid at the feet of the broader Canadian society, for the obstacles posed by societal discrimination and prejudice were immense. Government policy tried to induce Indians into a mainstream that was unwilling to receive them.¹⁹

Paternalism

One way to understand the word 'paternalism' is to remember that it relates to a father. Twiss defines paternalism as a policy or practice of teaching or governing people in a fatherly manner especially by providing for their needs without giving them responsibility. Paternalism is always a control issue. It is always an issue of superiority and condescension.²⁰

The fruit of Western paternalism, according to Hodges, is anemic mission churches that are not allowed to grow naturally in the soils in which they are planted. Early missionaries seldom understood their 'transitory' role, but rather became indispensable to the running of the mission.²¹

Colonialism

Colonialism is another word that frequently comes up when Native and non-Native relations are discussed. This is true in Native political issues with the federal government as well as in

---

[18] Ponting (ed.), *Arduous Journey*, pp. 25-26.
[19] Ponting (ed.), *Arduous Journey*, p. 27.
[20] Richard L. Twiss, *Culture, Christ, and the Kingdom Seminar* (Vancouver, WA: Wiconi International, 1996), p. 36.
[21] Gailyn Van Rheenen, *Missions: Biblical Foundations & Contemporary Strategies* (Grand Rapids, MI: Zondervan, 1996), p. 187.

Mission/Church relations. It is important then to understand what colonialism means in both past and present. The dictionary defines colonialism as (1) control by one power over a dependent area or people; (2) a policy advocating or based on such control.[22] Clearly, colonialism is closely related to paternalism.

> Robert Blauner identified certain basic components and indicators of colonialism. He saw such colonialism as beginning with the forced integration of the indigenous people into the dominant society on terms controlled by the dominant society. Second, under his definition of colonialism the colonizing power carries out a policy that constrains, transforms, or destroys the culture (and we might add, the economy) of the indigenous people. Third, racism as a system of domination (and a justifying ideology) is said to characterize the society. Fourth, the members of the colonized group are said by Blauner to be administered by members of the dominant power, especially in such a way as to be managed and manipulated in terms of their ethnic status.[23]

To Indian leaders the word 'mission' conveys negative connotations because of its association with colonialism. Verkuyl points out that impure motives have been clearly discernible throughout the history of Christian mission. He says one of the most frequent criticisms made of missionary work, particularly of missions originating in the West, is that it was done for imperialist reasons. By imperialism, Verkuyl means the attempt by one state to use another people or state as a means to achieve its own goals. Imperialism for centuries came in the form of colonialism, but it does not absolutely depend on political domination of another people in order to function.[24]

The question is, were imperialist motives present in the work of missions throughout history? According to Verkuyl, the answer is clearly yes. He writes,

---

[22] *Webster's New Collegiate Dictionary* (1976), s.v. 'colonialism'.
[23] Ponting (ed.), *Arduous Journey*, p. 85.
[24] J. Verkuyl, *Contemporary Missiology: An Introduction* (Grand Rapids, MI: Eerdmans, 1978), p. 168.

During the fifteenth and sixteenth centuries Pope Nicholas V and Alexander VI instructed first Spain and later Portugal to extend their political influence to Asia, Africa, and the recently discovered America, but also to be zealous for extending the domain of the Roman Catholic church. By so doing, these Popes tied missions tightly to political authority and to the work of the conquistadors who worked not only in the Antilles and in Latin America but also elsewhere to establish 'Royal Patronage' in the fifteenth and sixteenth centuries. The results of this are well known.[25]

Another impure motive Verkuyl singles out is ecclesiastical colonialism. He says that ecclesiastical colonialism is the urge of missionaries to impose the model of the mother church on the Native churches among whom they are working rather than give the people the freedom to shape their own churches in response to the gospel. Verkuyl's point is valid. Although with the advent of the twentieth century there is much more room for self-expression within the Anglican fellowship of churches, not every trace of this colonialism is yet obliterated.[26]

Bosch points out that the new world 'mission', is historically linked indissolubly with the colonial era and with the idea of a magisterial commissioning. The term presupposes an established church in Europe which dispatched delegates to convert overseas people and was as such an attendant phenomenon of European expansion. The church was understood as a legal institution which had the right to entrust its 'mission' to secular powers and to corps of 'specialists' – priests or religious. 'Mission' meant the activities by which the Western ecclesiastical system was extended into the rest of the world.[27]

Although we disagree with colonialism, at the same time, we cannot be too harsh in our criticism against the colonialistic approach to missions in the past. We have to consider the tremendous impact that the colonial era had on people in the Western

---

[25] Verkuyl, *Contemporary Missiology*, p. 168.
[26] Verkuyl, *Contemporary Missiology*, p. 173.
[27] David J. Bosch, *Transforming Mission: Paradigm Shifts in Theology of Mission* (Maryknoll, NY: Orbis Books, 1996), p. 228.

part of the world. If we had lived during that time we probably would have thought the same way.

Donald J. Jacobs writes,

> Modern Western missions coincided with the expansion of Western colonialism. Mission societies felt obliged to pursue a dual mandate, an evangelizing one and a 'civilizing' one. The interests of missions and colonizers blended on the 'civilizing' point. At the time the West was making major advances in medicine, technology, education, industry, and agricultural production. Those who were concerned with the civilizing effects of mission pressed for the introduction of programs that were unapologetically 'Western', such as formal education, medical programs both to prevent and to cure illness, improved agricultural techniques, industrial programs, structures for administering the new churches, and the like. The worldview undergirding these Western programs was usually in conflict with major facets of the local worldview. But that did not seem to concern the eager exporters of Western culture.
>
> The 'dual mandate' motif, when applied to local churches, meant that new Christians were expected to abandon their cultures and their worldviews. Becoming a Christian was synonymous with becoming Western.[28]

Protestant Missionaries

In the nineteenth century, Britain was the principal source of protestant missionaries and the main base of the missionary movement.[29] From 1776 to 1858 the Anglican and Methodist missionaries from England established numerous mission stations. Some of these men became famous for their missionary work among the Indian people.

---

[28] Donald R. Jacobs, 'Contextualization in Mission', in James M. Phillips and Robert T. Coote (eds.), *Toward the Twenty-first Century in Christian Mission* (Grand Rapids, MI: Eerdmans, 1993), p. 237.

[29] Andrew F. Walls, *The Missionary Movement in Christian History* (Maryknoll, NY: Orbis Books, 1997), p. 144.

Egerton Ryerson (1803 -1882)

Egerton Ryerson was a Methodist leader and educator from London, Ontario. He became a successful saddlebag preacher to the Credit River Indians. As first editor of the influential *Christian Guardian* and secretary of the Wesleyan Missionary Society and, later, first president of the general conference of the Methodist Church of Canada, he was probably the most influential Canadian Methodist of his time.[30]

Egerton R. Young

In 1868, Reverend Egerton Ryerson Young was pastoring a thriving Methodist Church in Hamilton, Ontario. He and his wife Elizabeth were married in December of that year. A few days after their marriage God called them to serve as missionaries among the Cree and Saulteaux Indians at Norway House, and in the North-West Territories north of Lake Winnipeg. The book, *By Canoe and Dog Train*, is Reverend Young's own account of the adventures, blessings, and hardships he and his family experienced while sharing the gospel with the Indian people of Canada's northland.[31]

James Evans (1801-1846)

James Evans came to Canada as a Methodist missionary from England in 1823 and in 1828 began teaching at the Rice Lake Indian Mission in Upper Canada. Ordained a Methodist minister in 1833, he went to the Ojibwa Indians and in 1837 published an Ojibwa grammar and translated extracts and some hymns into Ojibwa. In 1840 he became general secretary of all the Wesleyan Missionary Society's Indian Missions in the northwest. Extensive travel from Norway House made him realize the need for a written Cree language. After inventing a Cree syllabic alphabet in 1840, he published the *Cree Syllabic Hymnbook* in 1841 and organized a group of translators who by 1861 had translated the Bible into

---

[30] Robert Wilson, 'Ryerson, Adolphus Egerton', in J.D. Douglas (ed.), *The New International Dictionary of the Christian Church* (Grand Rapids, MI: Zondervan, 1978), p. 868.

[31] Egerton Ryerson Young, *By Canoe and Dog Train* (Prince Albert, SK: Northern Canada Evangelical Mission Press, 1991), outside back cover.

Cree. Opposition from the Hudson's Bay Company and false charges led to his recall to England and death in 1846.[32]

> Egerton Young in his book, *The Apostle of the North: James Evans*, writes, 'For long years after his death, there lingered scores of Indians in various places between York Factory and Fort Simpson, and from Thunder Bay to Rocky Mountain House, whose eyes brightened and whose tongues waxed eloquent, as they recalled him to memory. He was ever to them, not only Nistum Ayumeaookemow; but always the Keche Ayumeaookemow, the great Missionary that told them the good news.'[33]

Henry B. Steinhauer

One of the most devoted and successful of Indian missionaries was the Rev. Henry B. Steinhauer. In his book, *Indigenous Church Principles*, Kelly writes of Steinhauer:

> In 1840, the Wesleyan Missionary Conference in England was approached to send missionaries into Rupertsland and they immediately dispatched George Barnley, William Mason, and Robert Terrill Rundle to work in Canada under the direction of the Canadian Methodist Missionary Conference. James Evans was elected as the field superintendent, with headquarters at Norway House. As an assistant, he was given Henry B. Steinhauer. Steinhauer was, as far as can be determined by the evidence, a full blooded Ojibway who was born in Upper Canada in 1820. It appears that while he was little more than an infant, he came under the care of William Case. While Case was traveling in the States, a wealthy White man by the name of Henry B. Steinhauer, promised Case that he would entirely underwrite the education of an Indian boy if the boy was given his name. The young Native boy went to school, and by the time he was ready to work with Evans, at the age of 20, he not only was fluent in Ojibway, but he had mastered English, and Biblical

---

[32] Young, *By Canoe and Dog Train*, p. 362.
[33] Egerton R. Young, *The Apostle of the North: James Evans* (London: Marshall Brothers, 1899), p. 158.

Hebrew and Greek ... Steinhauer was a brilliant linguist who while still a young man, had translated into the Cree language the Old Testament from Job to Malachi, and the New Testament from Romans to Revelation. By the time he was 38 years of age, he spoke Ojibway, Cree, Blackfoot, Stoney, and English, and had control of the Biblical languages.[34]

Steinhauer had served for some years in northern Manitoba before arriving in Alberta in 1855. Setting up a solitary farm at White Fish Lake, fifty kilometres south of Lac la Biche, he gradually attracted enough Crees to form a self-reliant indigenous community.[35] Two sons followed in his footsteps.

Peter Jones

Peter Jones was a pioneer Methodist missionary in Upper Canada, of Welsh-Ojibwa parentage. He was born on the heights of Burlington Bay on January 1, 1802, and brought up by his Indian mother in the customs and ways of her people. For fourteen years he lived and wandered about the woods with the Indians in Canada and the United States. In 1816 he had the advantages of an English school, and was taught to read and write. After this he settled among the Mohawk Indians. In 1820 he began to attend church and to think favourably about the Christian religion. But when he saw the whites get drunk, quarrel, fight, and cheat the Indians, he thought the Indian's religion was the best. In 1823 he became acquainted with Seth Crawford who had moved to Grand River. Crawford was an earnest Christian worker who had taken a deep interest in the spiritual welfare of Indians. That same year at a camp meeting Jones was converted,[36] and later became an effective missionary among the Mississaugas, opening the way for the spread of Methodism among these and other Ojibwas.

John Sunday

One of the most remarkable conversions among the Indians of Canada was that of John Sunday, who afterwards was well known and justly beloved in Canada and England. For many years after

---

[34] Kelly, *Indigenous Church Principles*, p. 85.
[35] Grant, *Moon of Wintertime*, p. 146.
[36] Young, *By Canoe and Dog Train*, pp. 12-18.

his conversion he was employed as a missionary among his own people, and hundreds were converted through his instrumentality. He was very much sought after to attend missionary anniversaries. Immense crowds gathered wherever he was announced to speak. He lived a consistent and godly life, and afforded a glorious testimony of the gospel's power to lift up and save a drunken, lost Indian.[37]

The success of Indian missions was reported not only by the Methodists but also by the Anglicans. Grant writes,

> When Barnley left Moose in 1847 and the Methodists failed to replace him, the outlook for Protestantism in the area seemed bleak. With encouragement from the company, however, the CMS appointed John Horden to the post in 1851. He proved to be one of their most effective agents, becoming the first bishop of Moosonee in 1872. The most notable missionary who served under him was Thomas Vincent, a half breed who established a strong Anglican presence east of James Bay. Many people are surprised to learn that the Indians of northern Quebec are solidly Protestant, whereas a large proportion of those on the Ontario side are Roman Catholic.[38]

I was raised in Moose Factory, Ontario, and I often heard people talk about Bishop Horden. There is a public school named after him in Moose Factory.

In Upper Canada, the first Protestant Indian communities came into being not through missionary expansion but through the migration of groups already Christian. During the American Revolution most of the Iroquois fought on the British side, but there was some division among them that tended to follow sectarian lines. The Anglican Mohawks were unanimous in their allegiance to Britain, and so were some of those who came to Upper Canada. For the Mohawks who settled along the Grand River, where Joseph Brant was able to secure a large tract of land, Governor Frederick Haldimand built in 1785 the first Protestant

---

[37] Young, *By Canoe and Dog Train*, p. 18.
[38] Grant, *Moon of Wintertime*, p. 105.

church in Ontario.[39] This Mohawk chapel is still operating today as a museum, and as a special occasion chapel for weddings.

The Baptists were also active in the Grand River area, securing a foothold among the Tuscaroras in 1842 through the defection of another Anglican catechist.[40] The Medina Baptist Church is probably one of the oldest Indian Baptist Churches in Canada. It is located on the Six Nations Reserve on the outskirts of Brantford, Ontario, and has been in existence for over 150 years. Melchie Henry, a Native Indian, was the pastor of the Medina Baptist Church for fifty years.

From 1840 to 1890, there were literally thousands of Native people who put their faith in Christ, but after that the revival lost momentum and eventually faded out. Bud Elford, former General Director of Northern Canada Evangelical Mission, points out that one reason this happened was the failure of the missionaries to organize indigenous local churches. This meant that when liberal theology began to permeate the southern white denominations, it was only a matter of time until liberal ministers, sent north to be the 'praying masters', froze the life out of the dependent village churches.[41]

Indian Christians had been sharing the gospel with their own people, naturally spreading the word in their own way, and inviting a white missionary to come and teach them. In these early stages, the Methodists encouraged Indian leadership, recruiting and training Indian missionaries and teachers who had proved to be effective ministers among their own people.

The Methodist approach was that conversion could precede 'civilization'. But after the Indians became Christians, they were encouraged to assimilate into European culture.

> Neither Methodists nor Mississaugas doubted that civilization could and should follow. The Mississauga village at the Credit was reorganized in 1826 as a model community, with church, school, and European-style houses ... Village activities

---

[39] Grant, *Moon of Wintertime*, pp. 72-73.
[40] Grant, *Moon of Wintertime*, p. 79.
[41] L.W. Elford, 'Freeing the Slaves of Canada', *Good News Broadcaster* 37 (October 1979), p. 37.

followed a rigid daily schedule, and on at least one occasion [Peter] Jones made a cabin-by-cabin inspection.[42]

This illustrates the continuing paternalism and imposition of European values, leading to the failure to establish an enduring Indian church. By the mid-1800s, the emphasis was moving toward educating the children in mission schools:

> Certainly the very act of turning to children rather than their parents as the chief agents of acculturation left the Indians a marginal place in the missionary enterprise and discouraged the emergence of indigenous leadership. Never again would there be such a favourable opportunity for the inclusion of Indians as active partners in their own evangelization.[43]

The missions were effective in presenting the gospel, promoting education, and translating the Scriptures into some of the Native languages. But they failed to develop the kind of leadership among the Native people that would ensure a growing indigenous church. The Indian leaders who were active did not train the next generation to replace them. Dependency on the missions was encouraged by provision of education, housing, and medical aid with help from the government. This continued through the first half of the twentieth century.

Twentieth-Century Missions

As early as 1907 a series of Pentecostal revivals in Winnipeg drew many Crees from the north, some of whom returned to their people as ordained ministers. The Pentecostal movement has now spread into many different Native communities across Canada. Today the Pentecostal Assemblies of Canada (PAOC) claim to have over 100 Native churches in their denomination. In more recent years a number of other agencies have entered the field. Most of them are conservative evangelical in orientation, Baptist or Mennonite by affiliation, and American in origin.[44]

---

[42] Grant, *Moon of Wintertime*, pp. 77-78.
[43] Grant, *Moon of Wintertime*, p. 95.
[44] Grant, *Moon of Wintertime*, p. 201.

The ministry of Northern Canada Evangelical Mission (NCEM) is well known in Indian work today. Several years ago, I obtained a copy of a handout from the NCEM office in Prince Albert, Saskatchewan, which described the beginning and advances of their mission. Some of the information contained in the handout reads as follows:

> It was the mid-1930's, and spiritual darkness reigned in Canada's north. There is no record to be found of any evangelical work being carried on at that time. The work of the Methodists, that during the late 1800's had brought such blessedness, had lost its vigour, fundamental nature and evangelistic fervor ... In 1936, George Rainee, who was working at Gold fields, in northern Saskatchewan, became deeply moved by the sight of the bondage of sin of the Native people wherever he traveled. Although under appointment as a missionary to Africa, he took time to share his burden with concerned Christians across Canada.
>
> It was shortly after this that a rancher in Meadow Lake, Saskatchewan, area by the name of Stan Collie found Christ. With a heart burning for the lost he endeavored to go to Africa, but was turned down due to his age and the size of his family. Undaunted, he turned northward, and in 1939 caught a ride on a freighting expedition carrying supplies to outposts along the mighty Churchill River. What he saw that summer left an indelible imprint on his soul.
>
> He returned home, sold the ranch, loaded his family and belongings into a covered wagon pulled by four horses, and headed north. When the bush trail they traveled on came to an end, they traded the horses for a scow and sailed up Deep River to Buffalo Narrows where they settled ...
>
> In 1944 Arthur and Martha Tarry, along with their young family, left a pastorate in south-central Saskatchewan to join the Collies in Buffalo Narrows. In answer to the call for more workers, John and Hulda Penner also came north in the spring of 1946. Having sprung from a rural background, the work rather naturally became associated with the Canadian Sunday

School Mission. With expansion, there came a growing realization that this ministry to Indian people could be best performed under a separate organization. Thus the missionaries were led, in mutual agreement with CSSM, to establish an interdenominational mission board particularly devoted to reaching northern Canada's Native people ... In June of 1946 the northern missionaries met in Meadow Lake, Saskatchewan, and founded the Northern Canada Evangelical Mission with nine charter members and three mission stations ...

From humble beginnings the Northern Canada Evangelical Mission has grown to a combined staff of approximately 250 serving on 50-some stations across Canada, and in specialized ministries.[45]

Thirty years after NCEM was started, the Native Evangelical Fellowship of Canada, Inc (NEFC) was organized and later applied for a Charter from the Federal Government. This was granted on April 1, 1971. It gives NEFC recognition as a religious body which is able to operate anywhere in Canada. In relation to mission principles, I have always recognized the mother and child relationship between NCEM and NEFC. In fact, the five Charter members of NEFC, Stan Williams, Tom Francis, Albert Tait, Bill Jackson, and Everett Monkman were all at one time missionaries with NCEM.

---

[45] 'NCEM: Past & Present'. Unpublished paper in the records of Northern Canada Evangelical Mission, pp. 1-4.

4

THE BIRTH OF THE NATIONAL NATIVE CHURCH

Establishing the National Native Church

The birth of the Native Evangelical Fellowship of Canada, Inc (NEF) came about as a result of missionary endeavor to the Indian people of Canada. NEF's founder, Tom Francis, shares his thoughts on the formation of the Native Evangelical Church, as it was known in the beginning. He mentions that one of the early evangelical missions working in Canada among the Native people experienced difficulty in the proclamation of the Gospel because of cultural and language barriers. They came to the conclusion that if they were going to be used of God to reach the Natives and establish the converts, their whole missionary policy and strategy would have to change. That is, if God was going to reach the Native people, the Native Christians would have to do it. Thus the indigenous method was introduced.[1]

Francis observed that other evangelical Indian missions began to follow the indigenous method. As Indian men were won to Christ they were given Bible school training and encouraged to

---

[1] Tommy Francis, 'The Formation of the Native Evangelical Church'. Unpublished paper in the records of Native Evangelical Fellowship of Canada, pp. 1-2.

take Christian leadership. The Indian Christians grew in their faith and soon saw the spiritual need among their own people. Francis shares that these Native Christian leaders were encouraged to visit various reservations and villages of the north. Through their testimony and witness a number of Natives were saved.[2] Francis recalls the work of the Lord in one Indian village:

> The missionaries first went into Round Lake, Ontario in 1951. Round Lake's Native population at that time was 300-400. The Lord so blessed His work and the Holy Spirit so worked in the hearts of the people that within 3 or 4 years 3/4 of the village was won to the Lord.
>
> As Natives were saved, they in turn brought others to the missionary to be saved. As they were taught the Word of God, they, in turn, led others to the Lord.
>
> The Native Christians were taught the indigenous principles. They helped build the missionary's house and the chapel. The Christians elected leaders for their church and took part in the work of the church.
>
> Because of the Gospel: (1) Lives were cleaned up inside and outside; (2) Homes were cleaned up; (3) Yards were cleaned up; (4) Their debts at the local store were paid up; (5) The Hudson Bay Company trading store had to ship out tobacco and cigarettes because the converts stopped using them.[3]

The Lord gave Francis a good understanding of the indigenous church principles very early in his ministry in the 1950s. When the Native Church was still in its infant stages he realized that the indigenous teaching was needed and that it would encourage and develop stability, initiative, leadership, responsibility, contribution, and involvement. His reasoning followed the same line of thought as Harold Lindsell on the application of the indigenous principles. Lindsell writes,

> Let the national church train its own workers, set its own standards for ordination and for other church offices. Let it educate its own people for service and do it with its own money and

---

[2] Francis, 'The Formation of the Native Evangelical Church', pp. 3-4.
[3] Francis, 'The Formation of the Native Evangelical Church', pp. 4-5.

buildings and under its own church control. Let it send forth its evangelists and pay them and oversee their activities. And let it create other cells or churches which enjoy the same rights and privileges which it has been accorded but all in the fellowship of the saints.

When the indigenous principle is applied, the results will be surprising. The national church will be a stronger and more aggressive church. It will grow rapidly, and it will reach out in ever-enlarging circles to encompass the rest of the field. The relationship between missionary and nationals will be wholesome and brotherly, and it will open more quickly new fields of service for the missionary who has not become a nursing mother of a sickly child but the father of a mature and responsible adult who has grown normally and naturally from babyhood to adulthood in a framework of the New Testament pattern which is definitive.[4]

NEF began as the Native leaders were encouraged to meet together each year from various stations. This was encouraged by the Northern Canada Evangelical Mission and missionaries. The thought behind this was that such a meeting would bring great results. The Island Lake Bible School in northern Manitoba was used, since there were already a number of Native leaders there who were studying the Word. Francis remembers that these annual meetings proved a real blessing to the Native leaders. The people enjoyed: (1) blessings in fellowship; (2) sharing in testimonies; (3) discussing the work of the Lord; (4) anticipating the possibility of a National Native Church to improve the work.[5]

In 1957 the idea of having a loosely knit fellowship of Indian Christians across Canada was born. The Lord's leading was clearly evident as the Indian Christians from remote and distant areas were united in their desire to organize a Native Evangelical Church across Canada. During this time the Native leaders worked on the: (1) Doctrinal Statement; (2) Constitution and By-laws; (3) Name of the church – The Native Evangelical Church.

---

[4] Lindsell, *Missionary Principles and Practice*, p. 312.
[5] Francis, 'The Formation of the Native Evangelical Church', p. 7.

In 1969 the Board of Directors were elected for the young National Native Church. The same year at the General Conference in Winnipeg the members of the Native Evangelical Church changed the name to the Native Evangelical Fellowship. It was moved at the meeting that the local churches wishing to join NEF should register voluntarily at the main office in Prince Albert, Saskatchewan. It was also moved that a membership fee of one dollar be paid per member from each church every year. This would help build up the church fund for the executive work of NEF.

As soon as the Native Evangelical Fellowship had all the necessary documents ready, it applied for its Chartered Incorporation from the Federal Government. On April 1, 1971, NEF received its Letters Patent Incorporating under the official name of Native Evangelical Fellowship of Canada, Inc (NEFC). Through its Charter, NEFC has the right to purchase land, hold property, erect buildings, establish churches, etc.

The NEFC incorporates Native churches and individual members when they apply for membership and have been accepted by the Board of Directors. It is not a segregated organization but it was raised as a fellowship of indigenous churches. NEFC has always emphasized indigeneity as a means of reaching the Native people with the Gospel of the Lord Jesus Christ.

The NEFC can be identified as the National Native Church or the National Indian Church in relation to mission terminology. The NEFC is both a Native Church and a Native mission. As a Native mission it is able to promote missions and recruit missionaries. In his article on an indigenous church for indigenous people Len Cowan writes,

> The NEF, chartered in 1971, was founded by Cree evangelist Tommy Francis. The Board of trustees, entirely Native, today oversees 21 independent Native churches across Canada as members, with nearly 40 more congregations in associate membership.
>
> The size of membership congregations runs from well over 200 to fewer than 50. Many of the associate members are smaller congregations not yet incorporated as churches ... Several interdenominational mission agencies encourage the

Native churches they plant to join the NEF.

Besides the 21 pastors of member churches, the NEF currently has nine Native couples serving as full-time 'home missionaries' in Native communities. In addition, a number of associate workers serve on a part-time basis.[6]

After graduation from Briercrest Bible College in April 1980, my wife and I became full-time missionary workers for NEFC. We were assigned to help in the administrative duties at the Head Office in Prince Albert, Saskatchewan. In June 1981, I was elected by the NEFC members to the position of Executive Secretary. I held that position until July 1994. My understanding of NEFC's beginning and its philosophy of ministry are largely from the talks I had with my predecessor, Tom Francis.

After thirteen years with NEFC, one of the things I observed was that many of the Indian Christians associated with NEFC still did not understand the purpose of NEFC's existence. This is probably the major reason why NEFC does not have the prayer and financial support it needs so badly from its membership churches and individual members. There needs to be continuous teaching on the basics of NEFC's ministry until the members have a sense of ownership. Not too many Native Christians and missionaries have caught the vision of how NEFC as a National Indian Church can have an impact in Native ministries today.

Some Christians question the validity of bringing churches together. Some would even oppose the idea entirely. Melvin Hodges lists three factors which support the need for bringing churches together. He writes,

> First, the need for Christian fellowship. Small groups of individual believers that are cut off from all contact with other churches tend to become discouraged and inactive.
>
> Second, Christian unity and fellowship provide a stabilizing and corrective influence upon local congregations ... Contact with other churches serves to preserve a spiritual balance in the local congregation.

---

[6] Len Cowan, 'An Indigenous Church for Indigenous People', *Faith Today* 9 (July/August 1991), p. 23.

Third, overall organization permits the carrying out of specific projects that would be impossible for the local church alone.[7]

NEFC recruits and sends missionaries, prints literature, and distributes cassettes and videos. It holds a yearly national conference, local area conferences, family camps, and tent meetings for encouragement and shared ministry, and it provides counselling support for individual church needs.

NEFC as a Denomination

Even though it is first a fellowship of Indian churches across Canada, because of its incorporation, NEFC is recognized as a denomination in the eyes of the government. However, one of the ways NEFC differs from other denominations is that it encourages full autonomy for its membership churches. NEFC does not rule over the local churches in ecclesiastical hierarchy but it does have the right to approach a local church if there has been a violation in doctrine or by-law that each membership church has agreed to follow. Also NEFC's by-laws state that each member congregation shall be entitled to send two delegates who shall have voting power at the general meetings of the corporation.

The history of Indian missions reveals that the Indigenous people have been Christianized by several religious denominations. As a result of this there are some Native Christians and missionaries who are apprehensive about joining another denomination. For this reason NEFC has emphasized the fellowship aspect of its organization rather than a denominational aspect.

Is it valid for NEFC to be a denomination? From the administrative point of view, it is both valid and necessary. Once a local church becomes a member it can benefit from NEFC's national incorporation. NEFC will assist the local church to get its registration number for tax receipting purposes. NEFC has the right to ordain its clergy, and to recommend pastors and missionaries

---

[7] Melvin L. Hodges, *The Indigenous Church* (Springfield, MO: Gospel Publishing House, 1976), pp. 92-93.

for a license to perform marriages through Vital Statistics in the provinces where it is registered. As a denomination NEFC encourages full autonomy of its membership churches.

From a theological point of view, NEFC provides Bible teaching for the member churches and individual members through its Annual General Conference. Bible teaching and preaching are always highlighted at every Conference. In the past, the Conference selected various themes from the Bible that related to evangelism, discipleship, pastoral church leadership, and spiritual maturity. The Conference also had workshops and panel discussions on spiritual topics that concerned Native ministries.

Late in the fall, the NEFC sponsors an annual Native Pastors and Christian Workers Retreat in Banff, Alberta. NEFC uses the retreat for Christian fellowship and as a time of Bible teaching to the pastors and workers. These retreats have had biblical teaching on topics like spiritual warfare, indigenous church principles, and Mission/Church relations.

Also from a theological point of view, the NEFC requires that applicants for membership agree with its doctrinal statement. NEFC now has area pastors in different regions to stay in touch with the member churches. NEFC recognizes the autonomy of the local church, but oftentimes it will help Native fellowship groups deal with church discipline that may be difficult for them to handle on their own.

As a National Church, NEFC is there to help local churches in getting established, functioning, and meeting all legal requirements. The NEFC does not care to put its name on its membership churches because they rightfully belong to the Lord Jesus Christ. In his lectures on the indigenous church, Francis has often said, 'Give Christ the freedom to build His Native Church'.

Developing Leadership

Over the years a number of Indian Christians have received some formal theological training in both Native and non-Native Bible schools. Cowan writes,

When it comes to developing church leaders, the indigenous picture gets a little fuzzier. Several non-Native denominations and mission agencies run most of the Native training schools, and usually a high percentage of non-Native faculty teach the Native students.

An exception to the pattern is the National Native Bible College (NNBC), an independent Pentecostal school in Deseronto, Ontario. The ten year old school has a faculty of eight teachers, five of whom are Native. Current enrollment is 23; it has ranged from 12 to 30.

The United Church has a program of selecting and training Native church leaders that is loaded heavily toward control by the local congregations. A congregation recommends one of its members to the presbytery as a candidate for training in church leadership, and the presbytery arranges for the candidate's training through one of its two Native schools.

The Anglican Church has three main training facilities: Henry Budd College in The Pas, Man., the Arthur Turner Training School in Pangnirtung, N.W.T., and a Native Ministries Consortium run by the Vancouver School of Theology.

From BC to Quebec the PAOC operates six Native Bible schools. Each has a capacity of 12 to 20 students at a time. The typical student is a 28-to 35-year-old family person.

Each mission organization has some kind of leadership training for Native pastors. They often work in cooperation. The Northern Canada Evangelical Mission operates Key-Way-Tin at Lac La Biche, Alta., with an average of 20 students in recent years.[8]

The Indian Bible schools should take full advantage of using Native teachers to teach courses that are relevant to the students. This is important because the Native Church leaders need to sense and know that they have a key role to play in leadership training

---

[8] Cowan, 'An Indigenous Church for Indigenous People', pp. 24-25.

both in the local church and in Bible schools. The aim of the Indian Bible schools should be to build the Native Church.

The Native Church in Mission

At the 1981 NEFC General Conference in Winnipeg, Manitoba, Tom Francis shared his vision of 500 NEFC churches to those present at the business meeting. Francis told the Native believers that we cannot rely on missions alone to do this work. But with God's help, this is not an impossible goal for the Native Church and the missions to strive for.

Following mission principles, the primary purpose of NEFC is to see a strong, living, indigenous Indian church established by faith across Canada. NEFC encourages the indigenous churches to reach out to neighboring areas and beyond with the Gospel, believing that the local church is the best medium for evangelism.

In regard to the building of responsible churches, Gailyn Van Rheenen writes,

> The focus of missionaries and national leaders during the first ten years is on developing cohesive churches that, in turn, plant churches. The aim, therefore, is to initiate new churches in this culture, nurture new Christians to maturity, and train leaders in established churches. During the early years, much training is done informally as the missionary and mature local Christians model the doing of Christianity in their non-Christian context. The concepts of the Christian faith are intentionally taught, first through congregationally based Bible courses and later in small, yet appropriate Christian institutions overseen by national leaders. Over a period of years the missionaries make a transition from training evangelists and equipping young Christians to becoming trainers of leaders. Finally they begin to phase out their involvement in order to initiate another Christian movement. While the beginnings are slow (because missionaries begin as learners), the Christian movement gains momentum because people were intentionally taught,

Christians were nurtured, and leaders were trained in ways suitable to their culture.[9]

Many Indian fellowship groups today are only loosely knit. This is true even when the missionary has been there for several years. Melvin Hodges makes a valid point on planting an indigenous church as it relates to the self-governing principle. He writes,

> Local churches, properly functioning, are the fundamental units of the later united fellowship. If the missionary is able to organize his converts into local churches, then he has a powerful medium for evangelism and the essential basis for self-government. No matter how many converts there are or how many workers, if we have not enabled them to form themselves into local self-governing churches, then we do not have an indigenous church. The first step in self-government then, is the founding of properly organized local churches throughout the district.[10]

The past decade has witnessed some significant growth in the overall ministry of NEFC. Today NEFC is recognized as a National Native Church by many Indian Christians and mission agencies. The Native churches are growing and are more actively involved in the administrative affairs of NEFC. When I was with NEFC, I noticed that several Native churches were beginning to send financial support to the Head Office on a regular basis. If all the membership churches did this, it would give a tremendous boost to NEFC's financial needs.

A great encouragement for me was to see the indigenous principles being taught to missionaries and Native Christians. More and more Native Christians were starting to grasp the indigenous principles. With this understanding came support for NEFC's philosophy of ministry regarding the application of the indigenous principles. However, much teaching still needs to be done in this area.

The emphasis on indigenous principles teaches that the mission should build the National Church rather than just build itself.

---

[9] Van Rheenen, *Missions*, pp. 180-81.
[10] Hodges, *The Indigenous Church*, p. 24.

Some mission agencies have no problem accepting this teaching because they are serious in building the Native Church. The question that often comes up is whether each mission is willing to be a servant to the Native Church which is largely the result of its missionary endeavor. Van Rheenen writes,

> On his trips to visit field missionaries (Rufus) Anderson perceived that most mission efforts focused on social activities and failed to propagate the gospel. He discerned that the apostle Paul established local churches, each with its own independent presbytery, and from their inception these new churches were not dependent on Paul but immediately began to propagate the gospel in their areas. He concluded that 'missions are instituted for the spread of a Scriptural, self-propagating Christianity' ... Four activities would accomplish this goal: the conversion of the lost, organizing new believers into local churches, training a competent Native leadership, and guiding the church to become independent and self-propagating ...
>
> The role played by Anderson in American missiology is similar to that of Henry Venn in the English arena. Venn exerted great influence as the secretary of the Church Missionary Society of the Church of England.
>
> He perceived the stagnation of the mission churches established by his society and believed that 'spoon feeding' by missionaries created 'rice Christians.' He emphasized the need for true conversion, and this was reflected by the willingness of the local Christians to support the work of the church. He believed that the mission was like the scaffolding used by carpenters in the erection of a building. Once the building was constructed, the scaffolding was to be removed. But many mission works were like buildings that could not stand without the support of the scaffolding.[11]

The National Native Church is no longer just a dream and a prayer – it is now a reality. All across Canada, fellowships of Native believers are emerging and gaining strength and spirituality

---

[11] Van Rheenen, *Missions*, pp. 182-83.

maturity. As stated above, the Pentecostal Assemblies of Canada claim to have over 100 Native congregations. Len Cowan writes,

> The majority of Native churches fall into four groups: independents, evangelical denominations, mainline denominations, and Roman Catholic. Various 'Christian' cults have had little widespread impact in the Native community except for a strong Mormon influence in southern Alberta. The independents, arguably the most indigenous of Native churches, are represented by the Native Evangelical Fellowship (NEF) and various independent Baptists and Pentecostals. These are churches that espouse a Baptist or Pentecostal type of theology and worship – and may even use the word Baptist or Pentecostal in their church name – but have no affiliation with any denomination.
>
> Evangelical denominations include the large Pentecostal Assemblies of Canada (PAOC), Mennonite, and Christian and Missionary Alliance.
>
> Among mainline denominations, the Anglicans have had an active ministry among Natives, particularly among the Inuit. In some 195 Native parishes across Canada, the Anglican Church has about 65 Native clergy.
>
> The United Church of Canada (UCC) has some 44 Native churches from Quebec to British Columbia. In 1988 the UCC created the All Native Circle Conference, in addition to its regional conferences, but not all Native congregations have joined.
>
> The Roman Catholic Church has many church buildings on Indian reserves, but does not encourage particularly Native churches with Native pastors, according to Father Lorne Mackey of the Oblate House in Vancouver.[12]

In the early 1970s, Dan Kelly and Tom Francis were instrumental in promoting the indigenous church principles in Native ministries. These men were ahead of their time and had to pay a price for sharing something that was new and sounded controversial in Native ministries. When I joined NEFC in 1980, I also

---

[12] Cowan, 'An Indigenous Church for Indigenous People', p. 24.

began to emphasize these principles. The feedback I received from both missionaries and Native Christians was not always positive. But today when I share the indigenous principles there is a better response and more acceptance compared to twenty years ago.

Inter-Missions Cooperative Outreach (IMCO) is an association of Indian missions started in the early 1970s for the purpose of encouraging one another in ministry and developing a cooperative relationship to avoid unnecessary duplications. IMCO coordinates Native training under its missionary development program.[13]

NEFC is still quite young and therefore still needs the support of the IMCO missions. It is important for NEFC and these missions to have a good cooperative working relationship. Both parties need to show respect to each other to avoid Mission/Church conflicts. Dialogue should be encouraged to ensure unity and wholesome relations. Hodges writes, 'Anything which hinders the development of the Church, no matter how much immediate good it does, should be sacrificed for the slower but more permanent good achieved through the establishment of the indigenous church'.[14]

Since it was formed, NEFC has sometimes been misunderstood by some of the missions associated with IMCO. Some of the missions considered NEFC as just another mission and did not recognize its role as a National Native Church. In the early years of my ministry, the original idea of IMCO was for NEFC to be the National Indian Church. Later, as other Native ministries from different denominational bodies joined IMCO, it was natural to expect that they would not be too anxious to release their churches to NEFC. However, there were a few missions who still wanted to continue to release their churches to NEFC.

The diagrams on the following pages illustrate the relationships between NEFC and the IMCO missions, and the potential for expanding fellowship.

The big picture in Indian missions is the National Indian Church. In a sense, NEFC is the National Indian Church for the

---

[13] Unfortunately, after this book was completed, IMCO was dissolved.
[14] Hodges, *The Indigenous Church*, p. 117.

IMCO missions who plant churches and release them to NEFC. Ideally, the true National Indian Church would be more inclusive as a fellowship of all the Native churches. The truth in all this is that we all need each other if we are serious in our goal to build the Native Church.

NEFC and the Mission Organizations

1. The original goal of IMCO was that NEFC would be the National Indian Church.

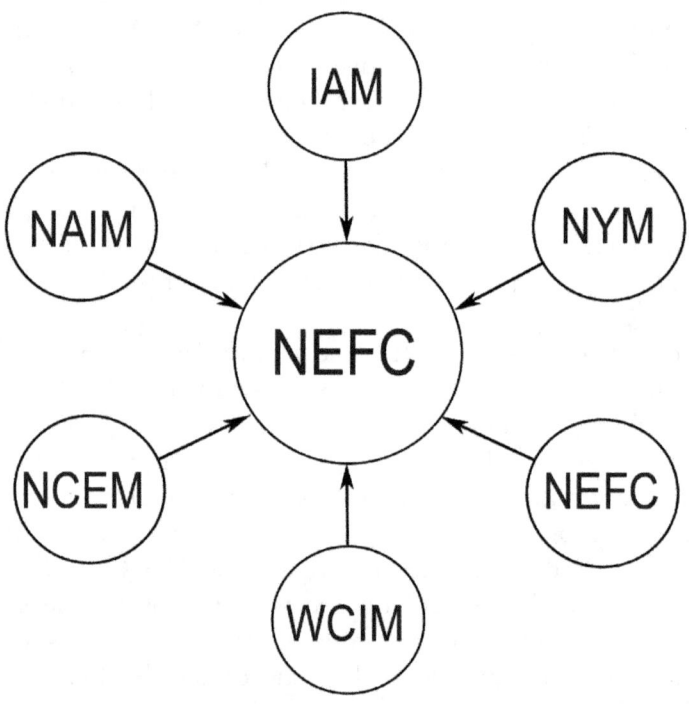

LEGEND:
- NEFC   Native Evangelical Fellowship of Canada
- IAM   InterAct Ministries
- NYM   Northern Youth Ministries
- WCIM   Western Canada Indian Mission
- NCEM   Northern Canada Evangelical Mission
- NAIM   North American Indigenous Ministries

The Birth of the National Native Church 63

2. As more members were added, IMCO took on a different structure.

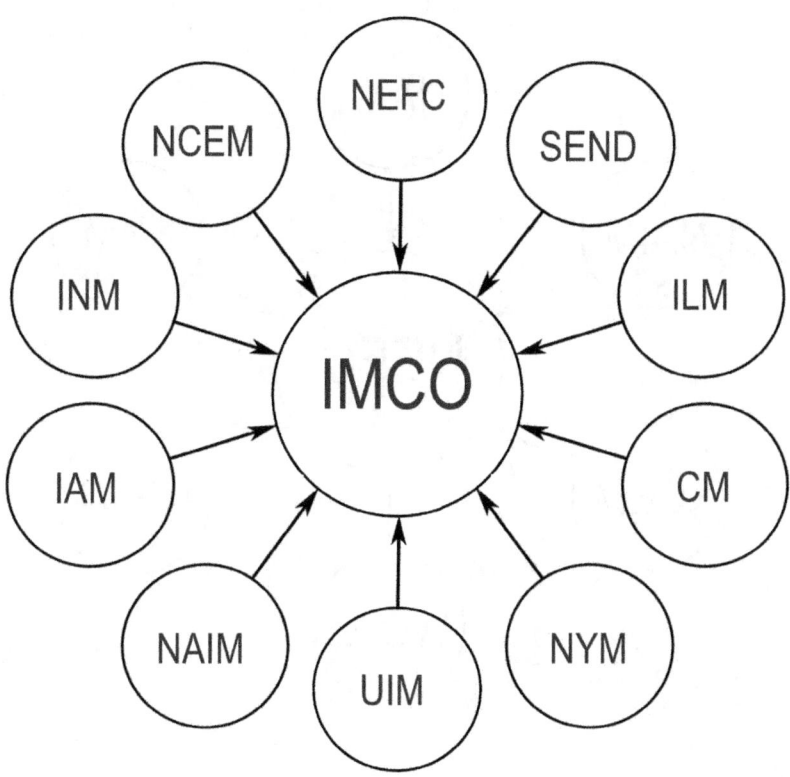

LEGEND:
- IMCO — Inter-Missions Cooperative Outreach
- NEFC — Native Evangelical Fellowship of Canada
- SEND — SEND International of Canada
- ILM — Indian Life Ministries
- CM — Continental Mission
- NYM — Northern Youth Ministries
- UIM — UIM International
- NAIM — North American Indigenous Ministries
- IAM — InterAct Ministries
- INM — Impact North Ministries
- NCEM — Northern Canada Evangelical Mission

3. This diagram was proposed for those missions who wanted to continue to release their churches to NEFC.

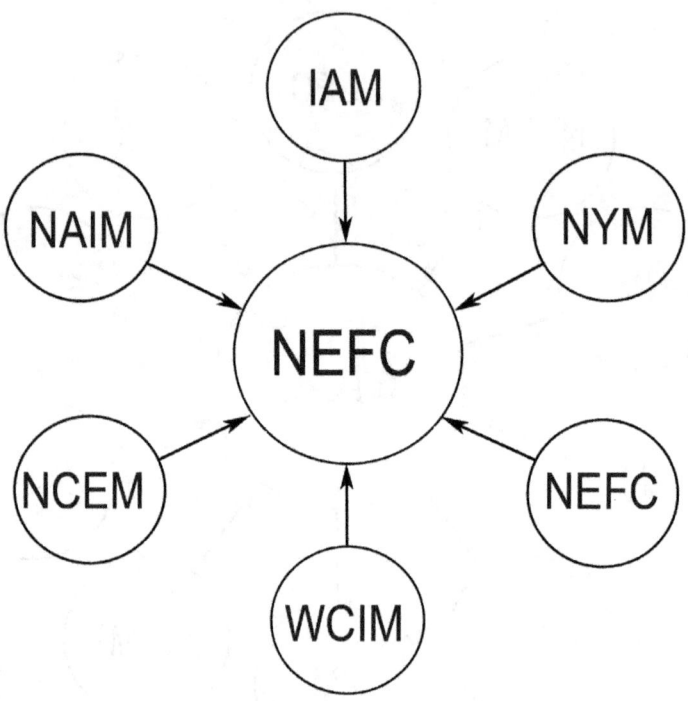

LEGEND:
    NEFC   Native Evangelical Fellowship of Canada
    IAM   InterAct Ministries
    NYM   Northern Youth Ministries
    WCIM   Western Canada Indian Mission
    NCEM   Northern Canada Evangelical Mission
    NAIM   North American Indigenous Ministries

4. The ideal indigenous National Indian Church.

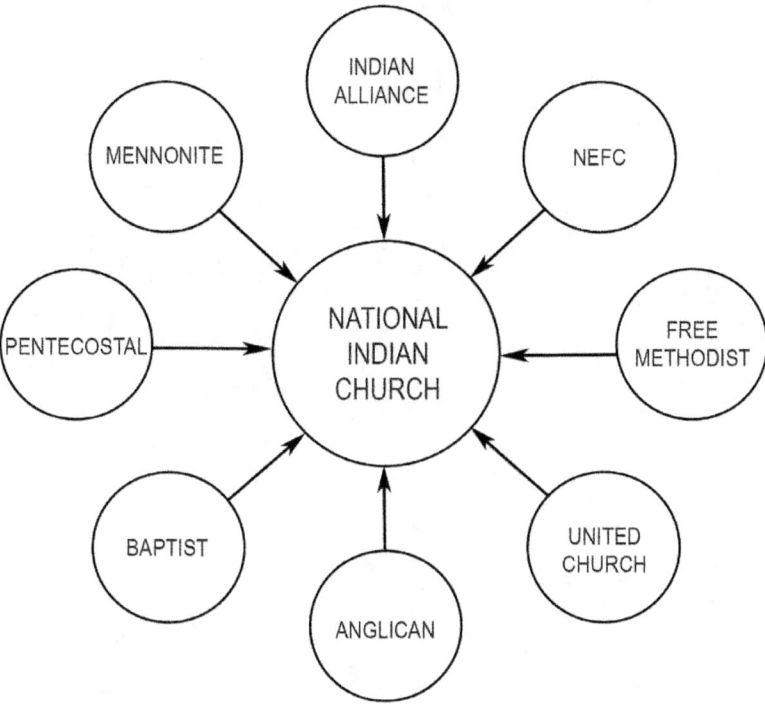

5

THE INDIGENOUS CHURCH PRINCIPLES

As we study the history of both home and foreign missions we find that missionaries in the past made many mistakes in cross-cultural ministry. However, we should not be too critical in our evaluation because we need to consider that they were doing pioneering work and did not have the missiological resources that are available today. We can learn from their mistakes and avoid them by studying mission principles in cross-cultural communication. The abundance of missiological resource material available can help make the work of the missionary more effective and far superior today.

Lindsell points out that a great mistake of western missionaries has occurred in connection with church planting. They were giants for the sake of Christ but they did not appreciate nor employ the indigenous method of church building except in isolated cases.[1] When they went into a village they sought to change the indigenous lifestyle of the nationals and conform it to their Western ways and Western superiority.

When missionaries built churches that resembled the ones back home, the nationals were made to accept something that the missionaries thought was a better way. The result was weak paternalistic churches and very few nationals were saved. The nationals

---

[1] Lindsell, *Missionary Principles and Practice*, pp. 295-96.

never felt it was their church and therefore did not take the initiative to evangelize.

Their failure to plant churches and to see fruit of their labours caused the missionaries to seek a way that would work. They discovered that they got better results when they involved the nationals by giving them more responsibility. Thus we have the concept of indigenous churches being planted.

The dictionary defines the word 'indigenous' as 'having originated in and being produced, growing, or living naturally in a particular region or environment'.[2] According to Hodges the term 'indigenous' when applied to mission work means: 'As a result of missionary effort, a national church being produced which shares the life of the country in which it is planted and finds within itself, the ability to govern itself, support itself and reproduce itself'.[3]

The Madras Conference of 1938 adopted the following definition: 'An indigenous church young or old, in the East or in the West, is a church which rooted in obedience to Christ spontaneously uses forms of thought and modes of action natural and familiar in its own environment'.[4] J. Herbert Kane makes this comment, 'If this definition is correct, the modern missionary movement has failed miserably to produce an indigenous church'.[5]

The goal of missions today is to establish strong indigenous churches. This strategy as a means of evangelism is emphasized because it has been proven to work in many countries of the world. The New Testament followed the pattern of church planting as is evident in the missionary outreach by the Apostle Paul.

The Marks of an Indigenous Church

In the 1840's, Henry Venn and Rufus Anderson, independently of each other, first formulated the 'three-self' idea of indigeneity.[6]

---

[2] *Webster's New Collegiate Dictionary* (1976), s.v. 'indigenous.'
[3] Charles H. Kraft and Tom N. Wisley (eds.), *Readings in Dynamic Indigeneity* (Pasadena, CA: William Carey Library, 1979), p. 6.
[4] Herbert J. Kane, *Understanding Christian Missions* (Grand Rapids, MI: Baker Book House, 4th edn, 1986), p. 351.
[5] Kane, *Understanding Christian Missions*, pp. 351-52.
[6] Verkuyl, *Contemporary Missiology*, pp. 52-65.

The three selves, as they are commonly referred to, are self-support, self-government, and self-propagation. Each of these must function in an indigenous church.

Self-support principle
In the past, foreign missionaries depended on the church back home and the mission board for financial aid. This was because the missionaries did not expect the nationals to be self-supporting. They never considered that in their natural environment they could support themselves. If the national Christians are trained to give, the church will be able to support itself.

Can a Native church be self-supporting today even though the poverty level is high nationally? The answer is yes! There are a number of Native churches in Canada today who have been self-supporting for many years now. These churches operate independently from missions and some of them pay their own pastor a full salary, support Native missionaries, finance their building projects, and take full responsibility for their outreach ministries. When the Indian Christians are taught to give instead of always being on the receiving end, there is no shortage of funds in the indigenous church.

Self-governing principle
It takes time to train leaders in the church because the new Christians must be taught the basic truths of God's Word. As the Christians begin to accept more responsibility, the missionary will gradually withdraw as a leader. In developing leadership in the indigenous church, a missionary should not hold a position a Native person can fill. However, the missionary still plays a vital role as an advisor.

Once the church is established, the missionary must be careful not to take the initiative in starting new programs or outreach ministries for the fellowship. As the need arises the Native Christians can do this. It may take longer but the end results will benefit the whole church. The key is to instill a sense of ownership in the minds of the Native believers if we desire them to feel responsible for their church.

Tippett writes,

> The only authority a missionary retains in a truly indigenous Church is the authority of the office to which the nationals appoint him or her. Then, the decision making should be carried out within a structure which is culturally appropriate. It should reflect in some way the accepted decision-making mechanisms of the tribe; that is, it should be something they can feel is their own. The greatest threat to an indigenous Church is the denominational character of Christian missions. We tend to plant denominational structures. Every missionary organization should be ready to fit the culture.[7]

Self-propagation principle
The main point of the self-propagating principle is that every believer should be involved in evangelism. This is accomplished by teaching the people to be a witnessing church. The Great Commission reminds us that every believer is responsible to propagate the gospel. Native Christians will reach their own people far better than a white missionary. They will do it faster and easier because they have the language and the culture. The missionary needs to encourage the Native converts to witness to their own people. The Christians need to be taught that they can lead others to Christ. The missionaries needs to multiply themselves by teaching others do the soul winning.

The six marks of an indigenous church
In his attempt to give a modern restatement of the doctrine of selfhood, Tippett lists six marks of an indigenous church:

> The first mark of an indigenous Church is its self-image. Does it see itself as the Church of Jesus Christ in its own local situation, mediating the work, the mind, the word, and the ministry of Christ in its own environment ...
>
> The second mark of an indigenous Church is that it is self-functioning ... A body which is dependent on one leader is not likely to stand on its own feet. The more people who are

---

[7] Alan Tippett, *Introduction to Missiology* (Pasadena, CA: William Carey Library, 1987), p. 379.

involved in a ministry of participation, the nearer the society comes to being a Church, and if those members are nationals, then it is an indigenous Church ...

The third mark of an indigenous Church relates to its self-determining capacity. Is the group an autonomous body, facing its own affairs as they relate both to the group and the group's outside relation? ...

The fourth mark of an indigenous Church is its self-supporting nature. This is the mark of stewardship ...

The fifth mark of an indigenous Church is its self-propagating fervor. Does the young Church see itself as being directly addressed by the words of the Great Commission?

The sixth mark of an indigenous Church is its devotion to self-giving. This is the mark of service ...

Now it may be said that these things are marks of the Church anywhere, and this is quite true. But they are the marks of an indigenous Church when the young Church undertakes them of its own volition, when they are spontaneously done, by indigenes and within their own pattern of life. When the indigenous people of a community think of the Lord as their own, not a foreign Christ; when they do things as unto the Lord, meeting the cultural needs around them, worshiping in patterns they understand; when their congregations function in participation in a body, which is structurally indigenous; then you have an *indigenous* Church.[8]

As noted in chapter five, I add to these marks the principle of self-theologizing. The indigenous church does its own contextual theology. My definition of the indigenous church is not limited to the self-hood principles only. First of all, I believe these principles are biblical and I agree with Hodges when he says, 'True indigenous principles are in reality New Testament church principles'.[9] I also like to include in my definition that the culture of the indigenous people has an important role in the function of an indigenous church. The atmosphere and the structure of the worship

---

[8] Tippett, *Introduction to Missiology*, pp. 378-81.
[9] Hodges, *The Indigenous Church*, p. 58.

service of an indigenous church should reflect the lifestyle, attitudes, mannerisms, and the cultural thought patterns of the nationals. As Tom Francis would say, 'An Indian church service should be Indianish'.

The Indigenous Principles in Mission History

According to Kane there are several major areas where the failure to adapt Christianity to the culture of the Majority World is evident. These points can also apply to North American Indian missions. Kane's lists of factors include:

1. Denominationalism. Missionaries exported their denominationalism to the mission field even though they had clearly stated that they would not do that. As a result the churches they reproduced resembled the 'mother' church back home.
2. Organization. They forced the emerging churches to accept their own elaborate form of church structure long before they were able to assume responsibility for it or to profit by it.
3. Architecture. They built churches along Western lines which were exact replicas of what they had at home. They built foreign churches with foreign money designed for foreign worship.
4. Worship. The missionaries followed the Western pattern where the worship is always on Sunday morning and the entire order of service is identical with that in the homeland.
5. Paid clergy. A church in the West must have a pastor; he must work full time and be fully supported by the congregation. He does most of the work; that's what he is paid for. This system of a one-man, fully paid, ordained ministry was exported to the mission field by missionaries.
6. Church discipline. The moral and ethical standards were those accepted in the 'Christian' West ... Discipline was often administered in legal fashion with little or no

consideration given to extenuating circumstances – spiritual immaturity, social pressures, cultural mores, etc.
7. Theological education. When Bible schools and seminaries were opened, they were patterned after similar institutions in the West. No attempt was made to adapt the instruction to the background of the students or the needs of the national church.[10]

As early as the 1800s, Henry Venn and Rufus Anderson started advocating the 'three-self formula' in missions. Both these men had great influence in missions and their ideas on the indigenous church were widely acclaimed. Verkuyl writes,

> Henry Venn was secretary of the renowned Church Missionary Society for 32 years and through this had a mighty effect on missionary thinking and administration in the nineteenth century ... Venn's name is usually mentioned in the same breath with his American colleague and contemporary, Rufus Anderson, who served as secretary of the American Board of Commissioners for Foreign Missions. In many respects their ideas are remarkably similar, though Venn's thoughts bear a definite episcopal stamp and Anderson's reflect his congregational background ...
>
> Venn's chief contribution stems from his vision of how young churches become independent. Both he and Rufus coined the famous phrase which has now become much misused and heavily criticized: 'the three-self formula.' The phrase means that the goal of Western missions must be to build churches which are self-supporting, self-governing and self-propagating ... He strongly opposed ecclesiastical colonialism which is more than satisfied to make carbon copies of Western churches in Asia, Africa, or among the Indians ...
>
> Rufus Anderson's influence lasted for one hundred years. Hundreds of missionaries came under his sway, and mighty transformations in mission policy occurred under his leadership. Old 'mission stations' were replaced by young churches, and Native preachers were trained and ordained to staff them.

---

[10] Hodges, *The Indigenous Church*, pp. 352-55.

Schools were used less as a means of evangelism and more as a means of training the laity. Young churches were given a greater voice in administrative affairs and decision making.[11]

In the 1890s, the development of the indigenous church in Korea was largely influenced by the missionary methodology of Dr John L. Nevius. He was instrumental in helping the church be truly Korean. He encouraged Christians, even leaders, to remain in their occupation so that they could serve their churches without charge. The structure of the church was to be just enough for the local congregation to carry, and only evangelists working away from home were to receive remuneration, and that only if the church could afford it. He also taught that the people should build their own churches according to Native custom.[12]

The first time I heard about indigenous church principles was through NAIM missionaries Dr Dan Kelly and his wife Jan. This was in 1978 while my wife and I were students at Briercrest Bible College. I took a couple of mission courses in Bible school, but I did not fully understand the indigenous principles. In the beginning I was quite defensive to my own way of thinking but gradually I started to listen more. Dan and Jan spent many hours with us until we began to grasp these important mission principles.

At Briercrest, one of the requirements for graduation with the Bachelor of Religious Education Degree was a major research project. Through Dan and Jan's guidance I selected the topic, 'How To Plant An Indigenous Church'. While I was writing this research paper I began to understand the importance of applying cross-cultural mission principles in Native ministries. Later, the indigenous principles would have a prominent role in developing my personal philosophy of ministry among the Indigenous people.

After graduation, I returned for another year of studies at Briercrest to prepare myself for further theological studies in the near future. During that school year in 1979-80, we helped to start a Native church in Regina, Saskatchewan. Right from the start we

---

[11] Verkuyl, *Contemporary Missiology*, pp. 52-65.
[12] Jacobs, 'Contextualization in Mission', p. 238.

applied the indigenous principles. Since not everyone understood the indigenous principles, there was a lot of explaining and teaching to do. However, the Lord blessed the work in Regina and we saw quite a number of Native people respond to the gospel.

McGavran writes,

> Indigenous principles are very popular. Properly understood, they have great value for the propagation of the Gospel. They are just as useful in Texas as in Tanzania and should be taken seriously by all students of church growth. Books by Nevius, Clark, Allen, Ritchie, and Hodges are essential reading to all missionaries and to many pastors.[13]

The indigenous principles are widely accepted today. Bible Colleges and Seminaries are putting more emphasis on cross-cultural communication studies because mission sending agencies now require their candidates to have a good understanding of cross-cultural ministry before they go into the mission field. As a result the missionaries are applying these principles and at the same time are teaching them to the Native Christians.

Having taught the indigenous principles in a Native Bible school and also at a Missionary Development Program, my conclusion is that it takes time to convert to indigenous church thinking. Missionaries and Native Christian leaders have to be taught the indigenous principles. Tom Francis realized this, and he always emphasized that we need to teach the indigenous principles to the Native leaders and missionaries. When people understand and fully grasp the indigenous principles, it is like a new revelation to them. One missionary candidate actually compared it to the 'new birth' experience. Arn, a Church growth specialist, shares his conversion to church growth thinking. I believe the same idea applies when converting to indigenous methods. Arn writes,

> My pilgrimage to Church Growth really started in frustration and dissatisfaction with evangelistic methods I had seen and been a part of in America. My search led me to the local church. The church is God's plan for making disciples and for

---

[13] Donald A. McGavran, *Understanding Church Growth* (Grand Rapids, MI: Eerdmans, rev. edn, 1980), p. 373.

winning a world.

I determined to bring any expertise I had into focus at that time. To acquire more expertise in Church Growth thinking, I visited the School of World Mission and Church Growth at Fuller Theological Seminary. When I inquired concerning resources and materials for American Church Growth, I found that Dr Donald McGavran and C. Peter Wagner were team-teaching a course applying world principles of Church Growth to the American scene. I immediately became a part of that group. As I listened and learned, I realized here was the effective approach to evangelism for which I had been searching. In those hours, I experienced my third birth – 'conversion' to Church Growth Thinking.[14]

Converting to Indigenous Church Methods

Sidney Clark has often stated,

> Dependence is not a good preparation for independence ... The best thing a missionary can give a Native church next to the Gospel is its independence. Anything which robs it of this ... is bad for the mission, bad for the church, and bad for the cause both represent.[15]

The missionaries in the past failed because they did not consider cultural contexts of the Native people. Today is a new era in Indian missions, and missionaries must be receptive to what the Native Christians are saying. Several years ago, Tom Francis, Charlie Lee, and Jerry Sloan, three well known Native Christian leaders in the United States and Canada, co-wrote a paper entitled 'Working With the Indian Church'. In their paper they mentioned that the times are changing and the attitudes of the Indian people are changing also. This paper was written over twenty years ago and at that time they were aware that there was a growing cultural and ethnic identity which approached a nationalistic attitude on the

---

[14] Donald A. McGavran and Winfield C. Arn, *Ten Steps for Church Growth* (San Francisco, CA: Harper & Row Publishers, 1977), p. 12.

[15] Kelly, *Indigenous Church Principles*, p. 110.

part of some of the Native people. This is exactly what is happening today.

These men clearly understood that methods of evangelism must vary according to the need of each particular village, reservation, or urban situation. They emphasized the importance of knowing the cultural and religious background of the people we are dealing with. They believed that the Great Commission involves teaching and making disciples and this requires the formation of indigenous churches wherever there are bodies of believers. They concluded their paper by expressing their desire to see among Native people indigenous churches which share the life of the community in which they are planted and find within themselves the ability to govern, support, and reproduce themselves.[16]

Hindrances to Conversion to Indigenous Principles

The indigenous principles are applied in Native ministries today but the process of indigenization has been slow. The indigenous methods in church planting are still quite new to some Native people and due to a lack of misunderstanding in mission principles there is some resistance to it yet. Another area that has contributed to the slow progress of indigenization has been the mentality of social dependency that some Native people still have towards the federal government and to the mission agencies. However, there are many Native people today who understand what self-determination means and therefore find no problem to accept the indigenous principles.

My first experience in church planting was being part of a missionary team starting an Indian indigenous church in Regina, Saskatchewan. This was back in 1979. One of the things I remember we did in our outreach ministry was that those of us who had cars provided a free taxi service for the Native people who wanted to come to our fellowship meetings. We picked up the people before the service started and then after it was over we drove them back

---

[16] Tommy Francis, Charlie Lee, and Jerry Sloan, 'Working with the Indian Church', unpublished paper in records of Native Evangelical Fellowship of Canada, pp. 3-6.

to their homes. Later on, as more people started coming out to the meetings and needed rides, the Native fellowship ended up buying a used school bus.

Shortly after our move to Prince Albert, Saskatchewan, the following year, my wife and I were involved in a church planting ministry there. In evaluating our previous ministry in Regina, one of the things we did not want to repeat was picking up people to come to church. We saw this as form of dependency on us and we honestly felt that if the Native people truly wanted to come to church they could find their own means of transportation. This approach worked because most of the Native people had cars and it was so encouraging to see them coming to church on their own. In the process of indigenization we did inform the Native Christians that we were applying mission principles in our goal to establish an indigenous church.

No doubt there has been a great work accomplished in some areas, work that seemed to flourish for a time, but when the missionaries left it gradually faded. This was largely due to the failure to apply the indigenous principles, and to a lack of teaching on the function of a local church. Francis, Lee, and Sloan ascribe the marked absence of indigenous churches to missionary paternalism. They also mention that another reason why there are relatively few ongoing churches is the lack of understanding of Indian culture by missionaries. The Indian people, in turn, have little or no concept of the local church, principally due to lack of teaching.[17]

Hodges gives four reasons why the missionary sometimes hesitates in converting to the indigenous principles:

First, perhaps unconsciously the missionary is reluctant to surrender the prestige and power which his present position affords ...
Second, the presentation of the indigenous church to the home constituency involves the loss of a certain popular financial appeal ...
Third, a sincere desire to show Christian charity by helping the

---

[17] Francis, Lee, and Sloan, 'Working with the Indian Church', p. 1-3.

underprivileged and relieving suffering may cause the missionary to cling to procedures that weaken the indigenous church ... Initial organizational plans and leadership may come from the missionary but ideally the material support should come from the local church and its environment. This is the indigenous method, the New Testament way. To allow foreign material resources to underwrite these features of the local church program is to weaken the church ...

Fourth, the very ability and efficiency of the missionary may strangely enough prove to be a hindrance to the development of the church. Impatient to attain certain goals, the missionary may use the direct approach instead of the slower, indirect approach through the nationals ... The missionary for instance, may be unwilling to wait for a national church to find the resources and make the effort to put up its chapel ... Or, in a second instance, the missionary may feel that he should continue to fill the pastorate of the church where he resides, because there is no national worker 'big enough' for the central church ... The trouble is that while there seem to be immediate results through following nonindigenous practices, permanent results are far more discouraging. And permanent results, those which remain after the missionary has gone, are the true test of his labors.[18]

Tippett writes,

The movement towards indigeneity is obstructed by methodological factors in the policy of the parent mission, and are therefore correctable – but only *through time*. Sudden home decision to force indigeneity on a young Church shows up thus:

1. A failure to develop an adequate evangel in the young Church, so that the removal of the missionary terminates missionary outreach.

2. A failure to develop an adequate operating leadership structure that will survive after the missionary withdrawal,

---

[18] Hodges, *The Indigenous Church*, pp. 113-20.

so that internal affairs drift and the community impact is innocuous.

3. A failure to develop stewardship dimensions adequate for local Christian action within and without the Church.

These weaknesses can only be avoided by a period of planned education (instruction and participation) *on the level of village congregations*. No Church can realize its selfhood without a sense of mission, leadership, stewardship and community responsibility. These are 'learned by doing'.[19]

Missionaries who apply the indigenous methods should assume their work as being temporary, right from the beginning. Their ultimate goal should be to establish functioning indigenous churches which do not require their presence but will operate on its own under the leadership of the nationals. Lindsell points out that missionaries must live their lives from the beginning among the nationals as though they were to have no successor, and even more as though they were able to relinquish all responsibility of their own, not at the age of retirement but long before that time of life approaches. He goes on to say that when they do this, the nationals will know that it is *their* church, and what is more important still, the non-believing nationals will recognize too that it is not a 'foreign' creation but one which belongs to their soil and to their people even though they may not be a part of it.[20]

About thirty years ago, Doug Taylor, a Baptist missionary who worked under the Northern Canada Evangelical Mission (NCEM), was used of God in starting the Cree Gospel Chapel in Moose Factory, Ontario. One of the Native men who came to know the Lord under his ministry was James Moses. Shortly after his conversion, James, who was single then, went to a Native Bible school in Cass Lake, Minnesota. After his graduation he went back to his home community and later became the pastor of the Cree Gospel Chapel. It was a wise decision on Taylor's part to move his family away from the community so that the Native church could

---

[19] Tippett, *Introduction to Missiology*, p. 390 (emphasis original).
[20] Lindsell, *Missionary Principles and Practice*, p. 299.

have the freedom to function on its own. Today, the Cree Gospel Chapel exemplifies how an indigenous church functions.

Evaluating the Indigenous Principles

There are some missionaries and Native Christian leaders who still find it difficult to accept and promote the indigenous principles. Their reasoning is that the indigenous methods focus too much upon mission theories of human origin. Finding biblical support for the selfhood of the indigenous church is a problem that often comes up.

Craig Smith, a Native American leader, asks the question whether the indigenous principles are biblical principles or primarily cultural principles. He indicates very clearly in his book that they are not biblical principles because Scripture shows not self-sufficiency, but rather inter-dependency among Jewish and Gentile churches. He also points out that the church was at its best when there was a plurality of leadership present that was truly representative of the diversity of the whole. His opinion is that the concept of self-governing implies that 'self' is limited to a specific cultural or racial group, and nobody outside the group need apply. Also, the issue of self-propagation implies that 'self' limits involvement to only those from within the culture represented. His understanding is that the homogeneous concept, where each cultural group works only among their own, fits this principle well, but it is hard to see this principle endorsed in Scripture.[21]

Verkuyl, in his evaluation of the 'three-self formula' of Venn and Anderson, recognizes its numerous strengths; however, he says the theory is somewhat lopsided and weak in several points. He writes,

> First of all, it is too ecclesiocentric. The Bible always relates the building up of the church to something much deeper and broader, namely the kingdom of God.

---

[21] Craig Stephen Smith, *Whiteman's Gospel* (Winnipeg, Man: Indian Life Books, 1997), pp. 73-74.

> Second, the note of self-support is accented so strongly in the theory that one would think it is the distinguishing feature of a true church. But the New Testament nowhere accords it that position of honor. On the contrary, it resolutely calls the prosperous churches to aid without grudging or reproach the poorer churches who cannot support themselves ...
>
> In the third place, the danger is more than illusory that the three-self formula could be exploited to justify a dismantling and severing of existing relations between churches ...
>
> One final criticism: while Venn and Anderson pressed for the building up of independent churches throughout the world, in the West they held that mission was properly the work of *missionary societies*, not churches. Their theory would seem to argue for churches to engage in mission.[22]

The primary purpose of the indigenous principles was to help missionaries plant independent churches in a cross-cultural setting. These principles contain many essential truths important to the missionary. Van Rheenen mentions that these principles challenged missionary paternalism and acknowledged the responsibility of all Christians regardless of social and economic heritage. It promoted a freedom that allowed local Christian leaders to develop programs and institutions that reflected the purposes of God yet were different from those of mission-sending cultures. It called people to Pauline principles of planting churches.[23]

In my personal philosophy of ministry, I recognize that mission strategies and indigenous methods are only tools and must give preeminence to the Holy Spirit. My understanding of the indigenous principles over the years has been progressive, and one lesson I have learned is the importance of looking at both sides of the issue before making a judgment. This is why I appreciate Van Rheenen for pointing out the following.

> It is easier to reflect critically on the three-self formula today than during the days in which there were no alterNative proposals. The most fundamental criticism of the three-self

---

[22] Verkuyl, *Contemporary Missiology*, p. 188.
[23] Van Rheenen, *Missions*, pp. 184-85.

formula is on its emphasis on *self*. Positively the word is an 'affirmation of identity.' Churches are able to operate autonomously, independent of their founders. Negatively, the term implies 'isolation, ceasing to be influenced and supported by others.'

From a theological perspective, however, no affirmations about self can fully describe a mature church. A church is never self-propagating but empowered and equipped by God to seek the lost. It is never self-governing but is ruled by the sovereign God and the Lord Jesus Christ. It is never self-supporting but provided for by God, the giver of all things. In a real sense Christianity is a denial rather than an affirmation of self ... The affirmation of self has meaning only when applied socially rather than theologically.[24]

One Native Christian leader once said to me that the reason why some missionaries have a hard time accepting the indigenous principles is that they are too 'spiritually' minded. And the tendency with Christians who are too 'spiritually' minded is that they rule out or deny anything that puts a strong emphasis on methods and strategies. The key is to have a balance in combining spiritual truths and the laws of logic. Charles Stanley makes an interesting point when he writes,

Part of the conflict we experience in trying to discern the voice of the Holy Spirit stems from a misunderstanding. Somewhere along the way we were taught that there is a conflict between what is spiritual and what is logical and reasonable ...

God created reality. He also created the laws of logic. Then He created our multifaceted brain with the ability to use these laws to understand and discover reality. The spirit world functions in accordance with these same laws. If it didn't, God would have no way of communicating with man. If there is a difference between spiritual reality and reality as we know it, how could God get spiritual truth into our spiritual world? There must be a connection of some kind. There must be a

---

[24] Van Rheenen, *Missions*, p. 185.

common bond, or the two worlds would remain mutually exclusive. God would not be able to communicate with man.[25]

You may not find much biblical support for the homogeneous unit principle; but in reality this missiological insight is valid and makes a lot of sense. The question that is often asked is, 'Is there a need for a Native church?' The answer is yes! One Native leader added in his affirmative response that this was not racism but showing wisdom in reaching people with the gospel. It is natural for any group of people to prefer attending a church service where the members look, talk, and act like them. Zunkel writes,

> Simply stated, McGavran's observation is that people like to become Christians without crossing significant linguistic, ethnic, or cultural barriers. People like to hear the gospel in their own mother tongue. They respond more readily, McGavran was saying, if it is presented to them in containers with which they are familiar and with which they feel at home.[26]

The Apostle Paul is probably the greatest missionary the world has ever known. What he was able to do in such a short time is astonishing. Roland Allen mentions in his book that in a little more than ten years Paul established the Church in four provinces of the Empire: Galatia, Macedonia, Achaia, and Asia. Before 47 CE there were no churches in these provinces; in 57 CE, Paul could speak as if his work there was done, and could plan extensive tours into the far west without anxiety that the churches which he founded might perish in his absence for want of his guidance and support.[27]

It is a well-known fact in missions that the Apostle Paul's most effective tool for evangelism was the planting of local churches. There is evidence of biblical support for the indigenous principles because, as was mentioned earlier, the three-self formula called people to Pauline principles of planting churches. In my view, it is

---

[25] Charles Stanley, *The Wonderful Spirit Filled Life*, pp. 208-209.
[26] C. Wayne Zunkel, *Church Growth Under Fire* (Scottdale, PA: Herald Press, 1987), p. 100.
[27] Roland Allen, *Missionary Methods: St. Paul's or Ours?* (Grand Rapids, MI: Eerdmans, 1962), p. 3.

obvious that the Apostle Paul's methods of church planting support the indigenous process because, as Allen says, 'He was always glad when his converts could progress without his aid'.[28]

The Apostle Paul's strategy was to plant churches in strategic points of the Roman Empire. He trained his converts to administer their own affairs and ordained elders in the church. He preached in a place for about five or six months and left behind him a church, not free from the need of guidance, but capable of growth and expansion. He was able to do this because he gave place for Christ. Allen writes,

> He welcomed their liberty. He withheld no gift from them which might enable them to dispense with his presence ... He gave freely, and then he retired from them that they might learn to exercise the powers which they possessed in Christ ... To do this required great faith; and this is the spiritual power in which St. Paul won his victory ... He believed that Christ was able and willing to keep that which he had committed to Him.[29]

I believe there is biblical support for the indigenous principles if these principles are applied in the local church. The three-self principles deal with church issues that relate to stewardship, leadership, church government, and evangelism. I have no problem accepting them as cultural principles too, because I can see how that would apply in making the gospel relevant to the cultural context of the Native people.

When Native Christians share the gospel with their own people, the result is a more effective presentation of the gospel. It is easier for nationals to reach their own people with the gospel because they already have the culture and language. I have seen for myself that the indigenous methods work and are effective in Native ministries.

When I was Executive Director for the Native Evangelical Fellowship of Canada, I visited quite a number of different Indian churches across Canada. It was encouraging for me to see that almost all the Indian fellowship groups had their own church

---

[28] Allen, *Missionary Methods*, p. 149.
[29] Allen, *Missionary Methods*, p. 149.

building. Some of them had a small congregation and some had a large congregation. One thing I noticed was that the majority of the Indian churches were indigenous in the sense that they were self-governing, self-supporting, and self-propagating. Many of the churches have been in existence for over twenty years and have operated on their own without dependency on NEFC or the Mission that first brought the gospel to them. Working out their own contextual theology is perhaps the most important task that remains for these churches. We will discuss what this means in the next chapter.

The indigenous principles are important today in Indian missions because they have been proven to work. The result of applying these mission principles has definitely caused the Native churches to be stronger and more aggressive in their witness for Christ. Native Christians are propagating the gospel in their own community and in nearby reserves in their area. Some Native Christians have even had an opportunity to share the gospel message in other countries like China, Philippines, Russia, New Zealand, Australia, Mongolia, South Africa, and even in Israel where Christ was born.

Johnny Whiskeychan is a Cree Indian elder from Waskaganish, Quebec. When he was a young man there was not much work available in Waskaganish so he went away to find work outside the community. He worked in a mine in Chapais, Quebec, for many years. During his holidays he brought his family back to Waskaganish to visit their relatives and friends. I was only five years old at the time but I can remember one of their visits during one summer. They must have brought in quite a bit of liquor by plane because there was a lot of drinking and partying going on that weekend. This gives you an idea of the kind of lifestyle he and his wife lived before they became Christians.

Sometime in his life Johnny must have heard the gospel message and the seed was planted. Later he and his wife became Christians and their lives were completely changed. Not long after his conversion, at a church meeting, the Lord gave Johnny a vision. He recalls seeing a picture of sheep grazing together and he noticed that one of the sheep separated from the flock and was walking towards the north direction. There was no mistake in Johnny's mind who that lone sheep represented. He knew right there that God was calling him to go back to Waskaganish and share the gospel with his own people. In obedience to the call of God, he resigned from his job and moved his family back to Waskaganish. This was about thirty years ago.

Johnny understood that Christ commanded his followers to go and share the gospel with others who have not heard the good news of salvation. At first it was not easy for Johnny and his wife Daisy to share the gospel with their own people. Some of the older people who knew them in the past and shared their old way of life made fun of them in their walk with Jesus. They were threatened verbally and persecuted physically. Their fellowship meetings were often interrupted by people who were drunk.

Gradually there was a response to the gospel, and the Spirit of God moved in a mighty way and literally hundreds of Native people got saved in the community. Today, the Waskaganish Cree Pentecostal Church is one of the largest Native indigenous churches in Canada.

The gospel which started in Waskaganish started to spread to the other Cree communities along the east coast of James Bay. It eventually reached some of my family members in Moose Factory, Ontario. A group of Native Christians from Waskaganish came to Moose Factory to hold house meetings. My late mother and older brother Allan went to one of their meetings and it was there they trusted Christ as their personal Savior. My mother understood the salvation message that night because she heard it preached in her own Cree language. Eventually my late father accepted the Lord and soon our whole family was saved.

6

DEVELOPING A NATIVE THEOLOGY

Self-theologizing: The Fourth Self

We are familiar with the three-self principles in the indigenous church, but most people involved in missions have not yet heard about the fourth self. This principle emphasizes self-theologizing which can also be referred to as the contextualization of the gospel. The fourth self is subject to controversy in missions because of its association with theology. It raises the question, 'Do national churches have the right to read and interpret the Scriptures for themselves?'

Paul Hiebert points out that most mission movements have led to theological crises. Three or four generations after a church is planted, local theologians arise and struggle with the question of how the gospel relates to their cultural traditions. How can they express the Good News in terms the people understand, and yet retain its prophetic message?[1] We see this process at work in the Native church today. Native Christians are asking about forms from their culture and about their meaning and function within the church. Someone asked Twiss this question:

---

[1] Paul G. Hiebert, *Anthropological Insights for Missionaries* (Grand Rapids, MI: Baker Book House, 1985), p. 196.

Can there be such a thing as a Christian sweatlodge? A pastor at an Indian church claims that God told him to start this sweatlodge. He says to leave your sins outside the door and then go in and pray to Jesus. If you don't pick them up when you go out, you are cleansed of your sins. I know this isn't right and doesn't line up with scripture. What can I say to refute this practice? Many people including pastors are getting involved with this. Thank you.

Here's my attempt to answer it. First let me ask, can there be such a thing as a Christian rock concert, Christian incense, or a Christian tipi? Is one architectural style Christian and another not? Can there be a Christian sweatlodge? What is it that makes something Christian or not? It is not the form or structures – but meaning or context.

Could there be a Christian sweatlodge in the sense that it is simply a place where some Christian brothers meet together to pray and fellowship with one another – while enjoying a refreshing sauna? As a structure, its intrinsic value is no different than a brick, wood, clay, or metal hut. Because it was used historically as a ceremonial house of prayer, is the form itself an object of idolatry? Electric guitars were originally manufactured for the sole purpose of playing carnal, fleshly, and rebellious rock and roll music. Why then are electric guitars used in churches today when rebellion is the same thing as witchcraft. Is there a cultural double standard here?

Could a pastor make the same statement about attending church on Sunday morning? The pastor says when you enter the sanctuary leave your sins outside the door and come into the presence of the Lord and pray to Jesus. Then he says when you leave if you don't pick them back up you are forgiven of your sins.

If they both mean that the act of entering a particular structure is what takes away your sin, then this is clearly a Biblical error. If they both mean that by confession of sin and repentance, and acceptance of God's forgiveness through the completed work of Christ, you are cleansed – and you don't continue sinning – then yes they would both be right.

My answer is a question. If there can be a Christian rodeo, rock concert, musical, sculpture, painting, church building, novel, clothing, can there be a Christian sweatlodge? If no, then why not? If yes, then why.[2]

In answer to these questions Hiebert says the solution is that they develop new theologies.[3] It is common today to hear of Latin American theology, African theology, and Indian theology.

As evangelicals we hold to the truthfulness of the Bible. We also have strong theological convictions. How do these two relate? Hiebert writes,

> At first we are tempted to equate the two. After all, our theology is rooted in our study of the Bible. Further examination, however, forces us to distinguish between the Bible and theology. The Bible is a historical document of God's revelation to humans. Theology is the systematic and historical explication of the truths of the Bible.[4]

Definition of Theology

According to Thiessen, the term 'theology' is today used in a narrow sense and also in a broad sense. It is derived from two Greek words, *theos* and *logos*, the former meaning *God* and the latter *word, discourse,* and *doctrine*. In the narrow sense, therefore, theology may be defined as the doctrine of God. But in the broad and more usual sense the term has come to mean all Christian doctrines, not only the specific doctrine of God, but also all the doctrines that deal with the relations God sustains to the universe.[5]

In contextualizing theology it is important to understand that there are two definitions of the term *theology*. Hiebert writes,

---

[2] Twiss, *Culture, Christ, and the Kingdom Seminar*, pp. 52-53.
[3] Hiebert, *Anthropological Insights for Missionaries*, p. 196.
[4] Hiebert, *Anthropological Insights for Missionaries*, p. 197.
[5] Henry C. Thiessen, *Lectures in Systematic Theology* (Grand Rapids, MI: Eerdmans, 1976), p. 24.

Sometimes we use the term when we talk about absolute truth. Theology is a systematic description and explanation of the way things really are, the way God sees them, and we will speak of this as 'Theology' with a capital *T*. At other times we use the term when we speak of human descriptions and explanations of reality that arise out of our study of the Bible. We will speak of this as 'theology' with a small *t*.[6]

Evangelicals are generally very cautious with anything that involves theology. This is why it is so important to point out that in the process of contextualization there are some fundamental Christian doctrines that never change. Some of these will be: (1) The presence and activity of the powers of darkness; (2) The fallen nature of human beings; (3) The revelation of God; (4) The person and work of Christ; (5) work of the Holy Spirit; (6) Faith; (7) The Scriptures; (8) The goal of disciple-making.[7]

The Meaning of Contextualization

Self-theologizing with a small *t* can also mean contextualization. In my understanding, the term 'contextualization' basically means finding new ways to make the gospel relevant within the cultural context of the people without compromising the essential message. I appreciate Luzbetak's simple definition of contextualization.

> We understand contextualization as the various processes by which a local church integrates the Gospel message (the 'text') with its local culture (the 'context'). The text and context must be blended into that one, God-intended reality called 'Christian living'.[8]

---

[6] Hiebert, *Anthropological Insights for Missionaries*, pp. 197-98.

[7] Viggo Sogaard, 'Dimensions of Approach to Contextual Communication', in Dean S. Gilliland (ed.), *The Word Among Us* (Dallas, TX: Word Publishing, 1989), p. 164.

[8] Louis J. Luzbetak, *The Church and Cultures* (Maryknoll, NY: Orbis Books, 1996), p. 69.

Muller brings out some good points about contextualization and the interpretive task. He mentions that the term *contextualization* points toward a new sensitivity to the problem of bringing the message of Christianity to bear on faith and life in the present. He mentions that the message of the gospel arose in one cultural, social, historical, and linguistic context, and we live in another. According to Muller the result of an effective contextualization of the Christian message is no more and no less than the adaptation of the substance of Christian teaching to a new linguistic and cultural life situation.[9]

Contextualization in Indian Missions

Contextualization is still fairly new to Indian missions, and to avoid confusion and misunderstandings we need to go slowly in our approach. There will be some resistance to it at first because our human nature has a tendency to resist or deny anything that is new or controversial. However, the process of contextualization might go more smoothly than we think, because the National Native Church has matured spiritually and I believe it is ready to handle this task. It is encouraging to know that there are some Native Christian leaders who understand what contextualization means and who have already taken the initiative to promote it in Indian missions.

The contextualization process will not be an easy task because it makes us evaluate our theologies and philosophies of ministry. We need to be open and flexible to any changes that we have to make. I appreciate the challenge made by Twiss,

> Are we willing to become weak for those who are weak, under the law for those in bondage, 'traditional' for the traditionalist and 'culturally relevant' like the Apostle Paul among the cultures of our own Native Tribes for the sake of the gospel? Can we use our liberty in Christ to go where lost people go?[10]

---

[9] Richard A. Muller, *The Study of Theology* (Grand Rapids, MI: Zondervan, 1991), pp. 201-205.

[10] Twiss, *Culture, Christ, and the Kingdom Seminar*, p. 43.

Though I am free and belong to no man, I make myself a slave to everyone, to win as many as possible. To the Jews I became like a Jew, to win the Jews. To those under the law (though I myself am not under the law), so as to win those under the law. To those not having the law I became like one not having the law (though I am not free from God's law but am under Christ's law), so as to win those not having the law. To the weak I became weak, to win the weak. I have become all things to all men so that by all possible means I might save some. I do all this for the sake of the gospel, that I might share in its blessings (1 Cor. 9.19-24 NIV).

What missionaries did in other countries during the colonial era is very similar to what they did to the Indian people in North America. In India and later in Africa, they rejected the 'pagan' beliefs and practices of the people they served. Consequently, the gospel was seen by the people as a foreign gospel. To become Christian one had to accept not only Christianity but also western cultural ways.[11] Canadian history shows that this was the same missionary approach that was used by Protestant and Catholic missions in Indian work. Quite a number of Indian leaders have taken Native studies in universities and colleges, and they look at Christianity as the white man's gospel and something that is foreign to them.

Because so much of their cultural customs and beliefs were rejected and erroneously taken away, Native Christians constantly face questions of how they can relate to their cultural past. How should Native Christians relate to medicines, dances, pow wows, myths, rituals, ceremonies, drums, and all other things that were so much a part of their lives before they heard the gospel? How far can the gospel be adapted to fit into a culture without losing its message? They have these questions because they are afraid to compromise with anything that may be directly or indirectly related to the Indian traditional religion. Dealing with traditions will

---

[11] Paul G. Hiebert, *Anthropological Reflections on Missiological Issues* (Grand Rapids, MI: Baker Book House, 1994), p. 76.

be one of the biggest obstacles to overcome in contextualizing the gospel.

I have noticed that Native Christians seem to be apprehensive towards some areas of their culture. This is largely the result of the western way of doing theology and it needs to be corrected. This way of thinking has also hindered the growth of the indigenous National Native Church. Richard Twiss, President and Co-Founder of Wiconi International, writes,

> By way of observation it seems to me there a measurable degree of fear in the minds of numbers of Native Christians concerning the place of culture in their Christian experience. If I had to guess why, I would say it seems to be the result of a lack of sound theological and missiological understanding of what Christ accomplished at Calvary and is supported by an aged and probably worn out paternalistic approach to missions among tribal people in North America.[12]

I agree with Twiss that we Native Christians are at times more afraid of becoming a stumbling block than we are of being willing to take the gospel to unbelievers for a witness. If ninety-seven percent of our Native people continue to perish without Christ each day, year, and decade, I believe Christian Natives need to re-examine our methods and approach to bringing the gospel among our people in more culturally relevant and therefore spiritually effective ways.[13]

Indigenization and Contextualization

As a Native Christian, I have often wondered if there were still something missing or something we were not doing in Native ministries. I thought this way because I did not see the results I expected. I give credit to the mission agencies for their emphasis on indigenization; but, in all honesty, we have not witnessed a bountiful harvest of Native souls. For years I taught and advocated the indigenous principles, but somehow I sensed that there

---

[12] Twiss, *Culture, Christ, and the Kingdom Seminar*, p. 44.
[13] Twiss, *Culture, Christ, and the Kingdom Seminar*, pp. 30-31.

was still something missing that would help make the gospel more relevant to the Indian people. I realize now that my philosophy of missions was mostly focused on indigenization, and due to a lack of knowledge I had failed to include the contextualization of the gospel.

I first began to understand the approach of missions in contextualizing the gospel back in 1990. At that time, I took a summer course on 'Christianity and Culture' at Briercrest Biblical Seminary. With a good representation of students from different cultural backgrounds, we had some interesting class discussions on the topic of 'contextualization'. This new insight in missions had a great impact on me, and I remember making a covenant with myself, that with God's help I would do my part to promote the idea of developing a Native theology for Canada's Indigenous people.

The term 'contextualization' means finding new ways to make the gospel more relevant to the people within their own culture without compromising the message. But before anyone can attempt to contextualize the gospel it is important for them to understand the culture of the people. Ultimately, the responsibility of contextualizing the gospel rests on the Native Christians because they understand their language and culture. If other national churches in other countries can develop their own theology, then our Native Christians certainly have the right to develop their own theology.

Contextualized Communication

If we expect Native people to understand and respond to the gospel message, it must be presented in a way that is concrete, subjective, and tangible. One of the principles in cross-cultural communication is that we should make every effort to present the gospel in such a way that it is understood by the receptors. God expects us to communicate His Word to be understood so that there is a response. Kraft writes,

> A receptor oriented communicator is careful to bend every effort to meet his receptors where they are. He will choose topics

that relate directly to the felt needs of the receptors, he will choose methods of presentation that are appealing to them, he will use language that is maximally intelligible to them.[14]

The means and methods used to present the gospel must be geared to meet the cultural needs of the Native people. Pentecostal and Charismatic movements are appealing to Native people because their theology and methodology relates to the way most Native people experience religious concepts. In his case study on 'Contextualization of the Church in Bali', I. Wayan Mastra writes,

> In the West, where most missionaries come from, religious truth is conceived in abstract terms. Church services are reduced to a verbal proclamation of the gospel. It appears that the western nations prefer theology which gives intellectual satisfaction; but in the East, people like religious experience in order to make their faith become real and not merely a theoretical conviction.[15]

When I was in Bible school, two of the courses I found difficult to understand were philosophy and psychology. One day after class, one of my instructors told me that because of my Native background, he understood why I had a hard time understanding the philosophy course he was teaching. I often wondered what he meant by that comment, but years later I realized that he had referred to the fact that the Western cognitive approach did not fully coincide with my concrete way of thinking. I agree with Hiebert that the Western ways of doing theology have been influenced by a Greek world that stresses highly rational and synchronic systems of thought. This emphasis on detailed systematic theologies is foreign to many societies.[16]

We constantly refer to the term *Western* when we talk about missions, but sometimes I wonder if everyone understands what it means and where it originated from. The term *Western* basically

---

[14] Charles H. Kraft, *Communicating the Gospel God's Way* (Pasadena, CA: William Carey Library, 1983), p. 7.
[15] John R.W. Stott and Robert Coote (eds.), *Down to Earth* (Grand Rapids, MI: Eerdmans, 1980), p. 267.
[16] Hiebert, *Anthropological Insights for Missionaries*, p. 214.

means the cultures that originated in Europe, were exported throughout the world in European colonies, and are now predominant in modern North America. It would include the worldview shaped by the Christianity of Roman Catholicism and Protestantism.[17]

In contextualizing the gospel message to Native people, it is important to know that the reality and activity of the spirit world is at the core of the North American Indian worldview. Native people in their traditional beliefs are familiar with spirit powers and spirit helpers which can either be good or evil. Missionaries working with Native people have to be prepared for spiritual warfare and power encounter with the spirit world. Wagner writes,

> The Pentecostal churches in Brazil go to the heart of the matter and recognize spiritism for what it is – supernatural, demonic activity ... Consequently, their evangelistic approach to spiritists stresses the power encounter; they are not afraid to pit the power of God against the power of Satan any more than Elijah was when he faced the priests of Baal on Mt. Carmel. Their message is that of 'Christ the Victor' and a common theme in preaching is deliverance from the powers of Satan. This is the kind of message that spiritists understand and respond to.[18]

Barney Lacendre, a Plains Cree Indian from Meadow Lake, Saskatchewan, was a hunter and trapper. He was also a medicine man. In his life story there was one year when he just could not kill any animals on his trapline. As a medicine man he knew where the source of the problem was. Someone had put a curse on his traps, and he knew that the only way to break the hex was to use another power that was greater. A missionary who gave him a ride into town prayed over his traps and also the bullets he held in his hand because he could not kill moose either. The curse was broken through the power of God, and Barney started to kill animals

---

[17] Adrian Jacobs, *Indigenous Christianity the Way It Was Meant to Be* (Belleville, ON: self-published manuscript, 1998), p. 9.

[18] C. Peter Wagner, *Spiritual Power and Church Growth* (Altamonte Springs, FL: Strang Communication Company, 1986), p. 127.

again on his trapline. This power encounter was instrumental in Barney's conversion to Christ. For many years before his death, Barney had a powerful testimony among his own Indian people.

Most Native leaders are aware that we are in a time of transition in the Indian work. Indigenization has been taught extensively in Native ministries over the years. The next step for Indian missions is to focus on developing a philosophy of contextualized ministry. I agree with Gary Quequish that to see this vision accomplished will require a broader perspective than just an 'indigenous Native church' movement. A Native church that is not contextual will most likely struggle on indefinitely, being irrelevant to its own community. This vision requires a philosophy of ministry that will be contextualized.[19]

Confronting Contextualization

The research I have done has helped me to see more clearly how much the Western way of interpreting theology has influenced Native people. The majority of Native Christians think that the only way to interpret the Scriptures is the way they were taught by missionaries. I agree with Hiebert that when a new church is planted, the first years are characterized by warm fellowship, emotional expressions of faith, and a concern for evangelizing relatives and neighbors. Most of the converts have simple theologies and accept with little question the theological teachings of the missionary.[20]

But in the Native Church today there are quite a number of emerging leaders who have been raised in Christian teachings and who are trained in a biblical exegesis. It is these leaders who are now raising difficult theological questions. Hiebert has observed that three or four generations after a church is planted in a new culture, local theologians arise and struggle with the question of how the gospel relates to their cultural traditions.[21] If that is the

---

[19] Gary Quequish, 'Effective Biblical Counseling Among Ojibway Peoples', p. 73.
[20] Hiebert, *Antropological Insights for Missionaries*, p. 196.
[21] Hiebert, *Antropological Insights for Missionaries*, p. 196.

trend in world missions, then it is all right for North American Native Christians to develop their own theology that will be more relevant to their culture and worldview.

As a Native Christian who has been involved in leadership, my greatest priority has always been to stay true to the Word of God. Before making a decision, I take time to reason things out carefully, especially when it concerns theological issues. I have no problem accepting the missiological concepts of indigenization and contextualization. I believe that Indian missions should be open to different methods and strategies that the Holy Spirit is already using in other parts of the world to reach the lost. I wholeheartedly agree with Twiss that there are views of and approaches to culture that need to be altered and changed in order to reach the ninety-seven percent of Native people who perish without Christ each year.[22]

When we think about it, most of us were raised in a church and taught to accept its doctrinal statement. We accepted one theological position and assumed that there was only one way to interpret the Scriptures, that all deviations from this approach were false. Hiebert points out that the first time we truly confront theological pluralism, we experience theological shock. As in the case of culture shock, our old absolutes are challenged, and the unquestioned certainties we hold are challenged. We are faced with the fact that there are different ways to interpret Scripture and forced to ask why we think our own interpretation is correct.[23]

If we do not have a background of missiological training, our initial reaction to theological pluralism is to deny it. This is one of the reasons why some Christians avoid the subject of contextualizing the gospel. In time, however, as they become more informed, they will face up to it and seek to deal with it. What helped me to deal with and accept theological pluralism was the understanding that all theologies developed by human beings are shaped by their particular historical and cultural contexts. All human

---

[22] Twiss, *Culture, Christ, and the Kingdom Seminar*, p. 6.
[23] Hiebert, *Anthropological Insights for Missionaries*, p. 197.

theologies are only partial understandings of theology as God sees it. We see through a glass darkly.[24]

Developing a Native theology does not take place overnight. It is a process that will take some time and we have to go slow in our approach. The concept of self-theologizing or contextualization is something that is new to most Native Christians, and so it is understandable if they have some questions about it. This being the case, it is very important that we be clear and substantiate whatever we say. Contextualization is debatable and subject to controversy, but it is a necessary step forward in Indian missions. Hesselgrave and Rommen write,

> Two dangers in approaching the task of contextualization – the fear of irrelevance if contextualization is not attempted, and the fear of compromise and Syncretism if it is taken too far. There is a need to use existing cultural forms that can be baptized into the service of Christ if the Gospel is not denied in the process. Unless this is done it is likely that only the surface layers of a culture will be changed. But since by definition contextualization appropriates indigenous linguistic and cultural forms, it always risks cultural and religious Syncretism. The only viable choice in the face of these two dangers is a contextualization that is true to both indigenous culture and the authority of Scripture.[25]

When I reflect on my theological background, I have to admit that the development of my theology over the years has been influenced largely by the western way of doing theology. I was raised in the Anglican Church, and later in life I trusted Jesus Christ as my Personal Savior in an Associated Gospel Church. For my theological training, I went to a non-Native Bible school and after I graduated my theology was influenced by white missionaries in Indian missions. In order for my ministry to be effective, I had to learn how to modify my theological training in order to make it relevant to the cultural needs of my people.

---

[24] Hiebert, *Antropological Insights for Missionaries*, p. 198.
[25] David J. Hesselgrave and Edward Rommen, *Contextualization – Meanings, Methods and Models* (Grand Rapids, MI: Baker Book House, 1989), p. 55.

It is possible that my theological background may have been a hindrance to me in allowing Christ the freedom to build His Native Church. I was bound to a western way of doing theology that was not fully relevant in meeting the spiritual needs of the Native people. However, God was faithful to bless my ministry. Today, I am searching for some answers to how Native Christians can redeem and repossess the cultural forms that have been taken away from them in the past. And I believe that one way to accomplish this task is for the Native Christians to develop their own theology.

Form and Meanings in Symbols

In the process of contextualizing the gospel one of the things that needs to be done is to clearly define form and meaning in symbols. Native Christians need answers to the questions they are asking about the drum, eagle feathers, sweetgrass, and sweat lodges. Twiss gives this concise definition and value of forms, meaning and function:

> Simply stated, 'form' is any material/physical object. Forms could be musical instruments, symbols or designs, articles of clothing, plants, or animals, etc. 'Meaning' is simply what an object means to a person or group of people. An object might have a historical meaning for one region or tribe and an entirely different one for another. 'Function' – based on its meaning some objects are believed to perform a certain function. In particular their religious or spiritual function ... This concept of form, meaning, and function is a core issue in understanding culture in the evangelistic and redemption process.[26]

Twiss points out that there is a great deal of misunderstanding and confusion concerning religion and culture. He asks the question, 'Can one separate a form and its previous meaning; especially where religion is concerned?' He answers his own question with this illustration:

---

[26] Twiss, *Culture, Christ, and the Kingdom Seminar*, p. 50.

Suppose a Christian enjoys the fragrant aroma of burning frankincense incense. They [sic] enjoy the fragrance purely for its ascetic value. Now suppose that they find it personally meaningful to occasionally burn the incense during their prayer time. For them, it brings to mind from these scriptures in Revelation, that symbolically and literally, their prayers are like incense that rises up to the very throne of God Himself for His pleasure. The smell and smoke remind them symbolically that through faith in Jesus Christ, God hears and answers prayer. Can you see anything wrong with this picture?

Now change the scenario and imagine that it is a Native believer who enjoys the fragrant aroma of burning sage, sweet grass, or cedar – in effect incense. Again, imagine that this Native believer is also symbolically reminded by the sight of the ascending smoke, and aroma of the burning cedar bark, that their prayers are literally ascending upward to the very presence of God. The smoke and smell is a symbol to them of the prayers of the saints spoken of in the Bible. Can you see anything wrong with this picture?[27]

Twiss points out that Christianity is loaded with forms, meanings, and functions. He says there is nothing 'Christian' about a cross. A cross was around a long time before the birth of Christ and was universally considered under Roman rule to be a symbol of human torture, suffering, and death. Yet, the shape of a cross (a symbol or form) has come to be identified with Christianity. He goes on to say that the forms themselves can mean something totally different to non-Christians. Turn the cross upside down and it takes on a whole different meaning for a Satanist. Take the olive (anointing) oil into the kitchen and it takes on a different function.[28]

Craig Smith in his book, *Whiteman's Gospel,* tells the story of a Navajo Indian Christian who could not sing a western style song if his life depended on it, but who could sure sing in a traditional Navajo chant style. He replaced the more than 200 medicine man

---

[27] Twiss, *Culture, Christ, and the Kingdom Seminar*, p. 51.
[28] Twiss, *Culture, Christ, and the Kingdom Seminar*, p. 54.

chant songs with Christian songs, praising the Lord, but in the same chant style he used as a medicine man. That is contextualization of the gospel as it should be.[29] In a similar fashion, it is well known that Martin Luther, and John and Charles Wesley borrowed some melodies of tavern songs and simply changed the words to make Christian church songs.

In contextualizing the gospel we have to be sensitive to retain as much as possible the culture, values, and customs of the people so as not to create a vacuum. Twiss tells the story that in Mongolia it is a common customary practice to offer a bowl of mare's milk to the spirit of the mountain as an expression of thanksgiving. His friend in Mongolia, Rick Leatherwood, told him that many of the missionaries told new believers they must stop doing this now that they were Christians. Rick challenged them, 'Why not?' Where in the Bible is there a prohibition against throwing horse milk? The problem was not the throwing, but the idolatry of offering to another God, so his friend has encouraged new believers to continue to give a 'heave offering' of their mare's milk, but now in order to give thanks to the God of Heaven and His Son, Jesus Christ. Twiss points out that this is a classic example of how a cultural activity can be transformed from its former idolatrous usage to become honoring to God through Christ, without disparaging Native culture.[30]

My personal view towards Native cultural forms and their symbolic meaning has changed considerably within the past couple of years. One of the things I learned is that I should not be afraid of Indian cultural forms or symbols. The problem is not with them, but what counts is that I give my full allegiance to God. As a result of this understanding, Christ gives me the freedom to be more inclusive and flexible in finding ways to make the gospel more clear and relevant to the Native people.

---

[29] Smith, *Whiteman's Gospel*, p. 128.
[30] Twiss, *Culture, Christ, and the Kingdom Seminar*, p. 32.

Steps in Developing a Native Theology

At first, I did have doubts and reservations about the possibility of Native Christians developing their own theology. I knew it would require the cooperation of many people in Canada and the United States who are associated in Indian missions. This was not something that a handful of individual Christians could do on their own. For this vision to become a reality, Native Christians and missionaries would have to set aside some barriers and make a concentrated effort to work together for the glory of God. It sounds idealistic, but if this ever comes about, the key depends on getting the Native Christians involved and giving them full ownership of the task right from the start.

Contextualization is not something new in missions; there is quite a bit of research material available on this. Another resource available to help the Native Church in developing its own theology is to consult the expertise of missiologists and seek the advice that may be given from missionaries and denominational leaders. I agree with Hiebert's point that churches in different cultures are part of a world community of believers. They, too, need to develop their theologies in discussion with that larger body. Although they have a right to interpret the Bible for their particular contexts, they have a responsibility to listen to the greater church of which they are a part.[31]

Guarding Against Syncretism

We recognize the fact that other Christians have the right to develop theologies that make the gospel clear in their different cultures. But a major concern that many Christians still have towards contextualization is the possibility of the national churches going theologically astray or going to the extreme into syncretism. We do have resources to test the truthfulness of our theologies and also to check against syncretism. Hiebert writes,

---

[31] Hiebert, *Anthropological Insights for Missionaries*, pp. 216-17.

> The first test is the Bible itself, for through it God has revealed to us knowledge of ultimate realities that we cannot gain by human experience alone. The Scriptures, not our theologies, are our starting point ...
>
> A second test is the ongoing work of the Holy Spirit instructing believers in the truth. We need a humble and open spirit that is sensitive to the leading of God in our study of Scripture. As one writer put it, we must do theology on our knees. We need also to recognize that the same Holy Spirit at work in us is also at work in the lives of other believers ...
>
> A third test is the Christian community. As priests in the kingdom of God, we have a right to interpret God's Word. As members of the body of Christ, we are responsible for listening to one another.[32]

Here Hiebert has given us three steps that help us develop a good contextual theology and avoid syncretism. The issue of syncretism is a great concern and is strongly opposed in Native work. Most people do not understand the term syncretism and it needs to be defined clearly. Here are some definitions that have been offered by various people:

> The union of two opposite forces, beliefs, systems or tenets so that the united form is a new thing, neither one nor the other.
>
> Syncretism is the attempted union of different or opposing principles or practices. Trying to marry two different and even opposing philosophies or religions. Without qualification the syncretist says that the assumption can be made that because the two are similar they are the same – synonymous.
>
> A distorted form of Christian faith, skewed by cultural and religious forces in the environment into which Christianity has come.[33]

Adrian Jacobs, a Cayuga Indian from the Six Nations Reserve in Ontario, tells the story about a traditional Indian religionist who said to a Christian minister, 'Your Christianity and the Indian way are like two railroad tracks. They head in the same direction. If

---

[32] Hiebert, *Anthropological Insights for Missionaries*, p. 202.
[33] Twiss, *Culture, Christ, and the Kingdom Seminar*, pp. 39-40.

you look to the horizon, the tracks come together. We are both trying to get to heaven. You go by the Christian way and I go by the Indian way.'[34] Adrian points out that the problem with this picture is that when you get to the horizon the two tracks are just as far apart as when you started out. It is an illusion. It only appears like they come together.

I fully agree with Hiebert that to make sure our theologies are sound we need three things: First, we need a careful exegesis of the Bible. This must include not only a study of the biblical texts, but also the historical and cultural contexts within which these were given. God revealed himself and his work to us, but he did so within the history and culture of a specific people. Second, we need a careful exegesis of our own cultural and historical contexts. Finally, we need a good hermeneutics in which the messages of the Bible that were given in other times and cultures are made relevant for the cultural environments of today.[35] In our homiletic classes we were taught to follow these same steps in our preparation of expository sermons.

Four Basic Assumptions of a Contextualized Church

According to Donald R. Jacobs, churches that are honestly seeking to contextualize the gospel embrace four basic assumptions:

1. A contextualized church is a church in which the basic needs of believers are met in Jesus Christ.

2. A contextualized church is a witnessing body. It employs forms, rituals, and behavior that are so relevant and immediate that their unbelieving neighbors receive an authentic and winsome presentation, through word and deed, of who Jesus Christ is.

3. The believing community will affirm those aspects of the culture which please Jesus Christ.

---

[34] Adrian Jacobs, 'The Meeting of the Two Ways' (Winnipeg: Indian Life Ministries, 1996), available from http://www.indianlife.org/twoways.htm, 1, accessed 8 February 2000.
[35] Hiebert, *Anthropological Insights for Missionaries*, pp. 201-202.

4. The believing community will identify and confront those aspects of culture which are detrimental and not consistent with the gospel of Jesus Christ.[36]

Native Christians should be excited by the idea of developing their own theology. It is a unique opportunity in the new millennium for Native Christians to work together as never before in reaching their own people with the gospel of Jesus. Contextualizing the gospel will make it more their own and no longer the white man's gospel. To make contextualization a reality in Native ministries, we will need prayer, humility, dialogue with others, counsel with wise brothers and sisters; and we need to trust the ongoing work of the Holy Spirit who is able to lead us into all truth.

An example of contextualization in practice is given by Twiss. He relates something that his family does to answer the question, 'What about feathers?' He writes,

> When my boys turn thirteen we have a special gathering of friends and family to honor them. We prepare a meal for everyone, and I ask several men and women who have an area of skill or success to say a few words of encouragement and challenge to them about their area of strength. We give them their first leather bound Bible with their name on it. We also give each of them a plaque with the passage from Isaiah 40:30-31 that reads, *'Even youths grow tired and weary, and young men stumble and fall; but those who hope in the Lord will renew their strength. They will soar on wings like eagles; They will run and not grow weary, they will walk and not be faint.'* And attached to that plaque is a beautiful and finely-beaded eagle feather.
>
> The eagle feather is a visual and symbolic reminder to them of the Biblical realities of youth and putting their hope and faith in God. Even from a distance, when they can't read the text of scripture inscribed on the plaque, the feature reminds them of the reality and truth of God's word, that if they put their faith in Jesus Christ, they can soar like an eagle in the midst of life's temptations and difficulties.[37]

---

[36] Jacobs, 'Contextualization in Mission', pp. 241-42.
[37] Twiss, *Culture, Christ, and the Kingdom Seminar*, pp. 53-54.

This is one example of contextualizing theology. Some other examples in the chapter include incense and prayer, Christian forms and symbols, Navajo chant style, and offering a bowl of mare's milk. Contextualizing is something that the church needs to do to be truly indigenous.

7

Cross-Cultural Communication

The Importance of Contextualization

The word 'contextualization' is widely used in the study of missions today. Missionaries must give attention to the importance of contextualization. According to Reed,

> the term contextualization refers to the sustained effort to present the Christian message in such a way that it becomes a part of the cultural context of the receptor people. It has to do with communication and may be considered the basic issue of cross-cultural communication.[1]

Bruce J. Nicholls defines contextualization as 'the translation of the unchanging content of the gospel of the kingdom into verbal form meaningful to the peoples in their separate culture and within their particular existential situations'.[2]

David Hesselgrave's definition of contextualization is more definitive and inclusive. He writes,

> Contextualization can be thought of as the attempt to communicate the message of the person, works, word, and will of

---

[1] Lyman E. Reed, *Preparing Missionaries for Intercultural Communication: A Bicultural Approach* (Pasadena, CA: William Carey Library, 1985), p. 138.

[2] David J. Hesselgrave, *Communicating Christ Cross-Culturally* (Grand Rapids, MI: Zondervan, 2nd edn, 1991), p. 136.

God in a way that is faithful to God's revelation, especially as it is put forth in the teachings of Holy Scripture, and that is meaningful to respondents in their respective cultural and existential contexts. Contextualization is both verbal and nonverbal and has to do with theologizing; Bible translation, interpretation and application; incarnational lifestyle, evangelism; Christian instruction; church planting and growth; church organization; worship style – indeed with all of those activities involved in carrying out of the Great Commission.[3]

The contextualization of the gospel message is evident in the New Testament. Hesselgrave, in his book *Planting Churches Cross-Culturally*, writes,

The Lord Jesus approached Nicodemus and the Samaritan woman very differently, and the emphasis of the Gospel of Matthew differs markedly from that of the Gospels of Mark and Luke although they present many of the same events. But perhaps the clearest examples are found in the communication of the Apostle Paul, who was commissioned to preach the gospel to various Gentile audiences. Notice the difference in his approach in the following instances:

- In the case of the monotheists in the synagogues of Damascus (Acts 9:20-22), Pisidian Antioch (Acts 13:16, 17), and Thessalonica (Acts 17:2, 3), Paul assumed a knowledge of God and special revelation and proceeded from there.

- In the case of the polytheists at Lystra (Acts 14:15-17), Paul emphasized the fact that the healing of the lame man did not mean that he and Barnabas were gods. Rather they were just as human as the Lystrans themselves.

- In the case of the pantheistically inclined Athenian philosophers (Acts 17:22-33), Paul began his message with

---

[3] Hesselgrave, *Communicating Christ Cross-Culturally*, pp. 143-44.

references to the 'Unknown God', a Greek poet, and nature and man as the creation of God.

Notice in the above cases how the gospel messengers built upon the previous understanding of their various audiences. 'Apostolic adaption' must be kept in perspective, however. First of all remember that the apostles did not change the gospel (Gal. 1:6-9). Second, though they used common concepts such as logos ('word', John 1:1-4) and pleroma ('fullness', Eph. 3:19), they invested them with distinctly Christian meanings. Third, cultural misunderstandings were countered and corrected (Acts 14:15-17; 17:31, 32; Rom. 3:28-30).[4]

Contextualization helps indigenous churches to grow. McGavran writes,

> Indigenous church principles, when successful, create congregations in which Christians tell of a good life possible to them and their listeners. When they explain biblical truth, they do so in thought forms and illustrations meaningful to them at their state of culture. To the people in high New Guinea, the pig is the supreme sacrificial animal. The Eurican missionary, though he may agree that it would be meaningful to say 'Jesus is our pig-sacrifice', can scarcely bring himself to do it. The Westernized New Guinea preacher, too, who reads his Bible, knows that John the Baptist said, 'Behold the lamb of God.' But the lay Christian, without any effort and with complete reverence, speaks to his fellows – Christians and non-Christians – about Jesus as the pig of God. Often the idea communicated may not be entirely according to Western notions, but it will commend the Saviour to those who have not yet believed, in terms they understand.[5]

Knowing the culture of the people is a prerequisite of contextualization. Hesselgrave writes that

---

[4] David J. Hesselgrave, *Planting Churches Cross-Culturally* (Grand Rapids, MI: Baker Book House, 1980), pp. 207-208.

[5] McGavran, *Understanding Church Growth*, p. 380.

once we have developed an awareness of cultural differences and the ways in which cultures operate, and once we have seriously studied the respondent culture, we can adapt to the new situation and contextualize our message without compromising that message.[6]

The core of Native culture is their traditional belief system. Sacred values are placed on their customs, traditional feasts, name ceremonies, dancing, symbols, legends and folklore, universal belief in the Creator or Great Spirit, nature, prayer, fasting, concept of power, and the supernatural realm. Missionaries have much to choose from the Native culture in contextualizing the gospel.

The Importance of Language to Communication

In cross-cultural communication, learning the language of the people is of primary importance to missionaries. They must learn to speak the heart language of the people if they desire their ministries to be effective. Charles Kraft writes, 'First of all, we need to be clear that *our aim is to learn the people and their culture, not just the language* ... the best way to learn the worldview of a culture is through learning the language. This is the most direct route into the heart of a culture.'[7]

The missionary needs to understand why it is important for them to learn the language of the people to which they are ministering. Charles Brock writes,

> A person's Native tongue is his heart language – the language of his emotions. When he is confronted with something so intimate as the life-changing gospel of Jesus Christ, he needs to hear it in his heart language so that it can permeate every part of his understanding and being.[8]

---

[6] Hesselgrave, *Communicating Christ Cross-Culturally*, p. 189.
[7] Charles H. Kraft, *Anthropology for Christian Witness* (Maryknoll, NY: Orbis Books, 1995), p. 250 (emphasis original).
[8] Charles Brock, *The Principles and Practice of Indigenous Church Planting* (Nashville, TN: Broadman Press, 1981), p. 40.

Hesselgrave points out that 'when it comes to learning the language of their adopted cultures, missionaries would certainly rate high among the various categories of internationals who have learned the language of their host countries'.[9] Learning the language is essential, but it seems this is an area also where many missionaries begin to stumble.

The English language is probably the most common language spoken by Canada's Indian people today. Many Indian people are bilingual because they learned English as a second language largely through the education system. However, there are many who speak only English because they have forgotten their Native language or never learned it at all from their parents.

If there are so many Indian people who speak English fluently then some missionaries might be inclined to excuse themselves from the responsibility of learning Native languages. But we need to keep in mind that there are still quite a number of Native people today, especially in the northern communities, who do not understand English. Missionaries who cannot speak the language of their host people must use an interpreter in order to communicate with them.

Native people in various communities today emphasize the importance of preserving their language. Promotion of the Native language has been successful among the Crees along the east coast and interior of James Bay. It is very encouraging to hear the little children speaking their Cree language in normal day to day activities.

In many countries of the world it is not uncommon for some people to speak two, three, or four languages. Among the Crees in northern Quebec, quite a number of Indian people are fluent in Cree, English, and French. If the Cree, both children and adults, can learn three languages, then the missionary should be able to learn another language also. Motivation is one of the keys to learning languages. In order to become fluent in another language there is no substitute for working at it. Not only is language learning hard work, but it is a time-consuming process. One of the most common excuses for failure to learn a language is lack

---

[9] Hesselgrave, *Communicating Christ Cross-Culturally*, p. 351.

of time. Focusing entirely on their 'work', missionaries often do not allow sufficient time for adequate language learning.

One of the most effective ways to communicate Christ's love to a people group is to know them first. The key to that knowledge is to speak their language. A white missionary who tries hard to learn the language makes a good impression on the Native people. The missionary who has a burden to minister to the real needs of the people will make an effort to learn and speak the heart language of the people. Not only must the missionary speak the language of the people but he/she must also be able to relate to their way of life. Brock says,

> He must immerse himself in the culture of those he hopes to win. He can only bring about spiritual change as he is able to relate to people. The planter must live within the culture of those to whom he is ministering. He must adapt to new ways. His mission is not to change culture. His mission is to lead people to Christ who will change hearts, which in turn will influence culture.[10]

Language learning involves effort, discipline, and close identification with the indigenous people. Reed quotes this story from Eugene A. Nida:

> Linguistic training is of great help, but it is no substitute for cultural submersion. One Indian who had been trying very hard to teach a missionary the indigenous language explained with great distress, 'I do not know what to do. I have been teaching this missionary for a long time, but she just sits and studies, and seems to learn nothing. Why, a Spanish-speaking girl married one of the Indians in our village, and now in one year's time she talks very well. Why is the missionary ignorant?'[11]

The problem is not one of ignorance, but of cultural

---

[10] Brock, *The Principles and Practice of Indigenous Church Planting*, p. 44.
[11] Reed, *Preparing Missionaries for Intercultural Communication*, p. 77.

isolation, of learning a great deal about the language but not learning the language, of studying but not speaking.[12]

The key to knowing people has been and will always be the language. Hesselgrave writes,

> Almost without exception, missionaries will be well advised to learn the language of their respondent culture ... Those who remain unconvinced should recall that when Paul was the center of a great controversy in Jerusalem, he gained the ear of the Roman commander by speaking in Greek and the attention of the large uproarious crowd of Jews by speaking in Hebrew (Acts 21:37, 40; 22:2).[13]

Lyman E. Reed points out that 'sharing Christ with the people of another culture and in their national language is the supreme purpose of missionary endeavour. The missionary should strive for that goal and realize that fluency in the language is one of the keys to achievement.'[14]

The Role of Culture In Communication

Kraft points out that language is the primary vehicle of culture.

> The final thing we want to say about language as a vehicle for culture is that it is the primary means of enculturation or socialization – the process by means of which children learn to be and behave as adults. Children are pressed into the worldview of their culture primarily through their language.[15]

Everybody in the world belongs to a cultural group. Hesselgrave writes,

> When babies are born into the world, they are at the same time born into one of its cultures. Over a period of time they become enculturated into the ways of that particular culture ... When a person moves out of the culture in which he or she

---

[12] Reed, *Preparing Missionaries for Intercultural Communication*, p. 77.
[13] Hesselgrave, *Communicating Christ Cross-Culturally*, p. 355.
[14] Reed, *Preparing Missionaries for Intercultural Communication*, p. 78.
[15] Kraft, *Anthropology For Christian Witness*, p. 250.

was enculturated and learns another culture, we say that he or she has be acculturated into that second culture and is therefore bicultural.[16]

The word 'culture' is difficult to define because it is a very inclusive term. Regarding culture, Pentecost writes,

> To understand man is to understand his culture – his language, his logic, his mentality, his expressions, his manner of life, his environment, and his worldview – for all of these entities influence man and his makeup. It is through culture that concepts are perceived, and in culture that religion in particular is practiced.[17]

Pentecost goes on to say,

> Culture is that reference point which gives direction to life. If those reference points are destroyed man is left to drift on a sea of insecurity. To destroy culture is to destroy a way of life or design of living. To divest man of his culture without offering a functional substitute is to place man into a vacuum where he finds only frustration. Cultural interrelationships are vital to man.[18]

Lingenfelter and Mayers define and explain culture as follows:

> Culture is basically a set of conceptual tools that people use to adapt to their environment and to order their lives in the pursuit of food, shelter, and family and community relationships. Each culture is the product of peculiar historical forces that have served to define a people's uniqueness and their personal and group identities. While every culture is imperfect and may be used by individuals in it for good or evil purposes, each one is the integrating point of reference by which people comprehend themselves and others. So if we are to minister successfully to the members of a different society, we must learn about

---

[16] Hesselgrave, *Communicating Christ Cross-Culturally*, pp. 102-103.
[17] Pentecost, *Issues in Missiology*, p. 79.
[18] Pentecost, *Issues in Missiology*, p. 79.

and participate in their culture; we must even learn to do things in their way rather than our own.[19]

One of the first things that cross-cultural communicators must recognize is that differences exist between cultures. They also must learn to appreciate all cultures as being equal. The myth of cultural superiority has been one of the major obstacles to effective cross-cultural communication. Hiebert writes,

> Cross-cultural confusion on the cognitive level leads to misunderstandings, but on the affective level it leads to 'ethnocentrism', the normal emotional response people have when they confront other cultures for the first time. They have the feeling that their culture is civilized and that others are primitive and backward. This response has to do with attitudes, not with understandings.
>
> The root of ethnocentrism is our human tendency to respond to other people's ways by using our own affective assumptions, and to reinforce these responses with deep feelings of approval or disapproval. When we are confronted by another culture, our own is called into question. Our defense is to avoid the issue by concluding that our culture is better and other people are less civilized.
>
> But ethnocentrism is a two-way street. We feel that people in other cultures are primitive, and they judge us to be uncivilized. This can be seen by way of an illustration. Some North Americans were hosting a visiting Indian scholar at a restaurant, when one of them who had never been abroad asked the inevitable question, 'Do you really eat with your fingers in India?' Implicit in his question, of course, was his cultural attitude that eating with one's fingers is crude and dirty. North Americans may use fingers for carrot sticks, potato chips, and sandwiches, but never for mashed potatoes and gravy, or T-bone steaks. The Indian scholar replied, 'You know, in India we look at it differently than you do. I always wash my hands carefully

---

[19] Sherwood G. Lingenfelter and Marvin K. Mayers, *Ministering Cross-Culturally* (Grand Rapids, MI: Baker Book House, 1986), p. 122.

before I eat, and I only use my right hand. And besides, my fingers have never been in anyone's mouth. When I look at a fork or spoon, I often wonder how many other strangers have already had them in their mouths!'

Ethnocentrism occurs wherever cultural differences are found ... The solution to ethnocentrism is empathy. We need to appreciate other cultures and their ways ... One way to overcome ethnocentrism is to be learners in the culture to which we go, for our self-centeredness is often rooted in our ignorance of others. Another is to deal with the philosophical questions raised by cultural pluralism ... A third way to overcome ethnocentrism is to avoid stereotyping people in other cultures, but rather to see them as human beings like ourselves. The recognition of our common humanity bridges the differences that divide us. Finally, we need to remember that people love their own cultures, and if we wish to reach them, we must do so within the context of those cultures.[20]

Native people understand the importance of keeping their cultural identity. There are a number of programs available on the reserve and urban centres which are designed to help Native people preserve their cultural values. Alan Tippett, a well-known missiologist writes,

Scripture and anthropology seem to be in step in recognizing the importance of diversity in unity; which suggests that the true meaning of integration is discovering how blacks and whites, Europeans and Africans, can live and work together without giving up their cultural identity.[21]

What Native people need to understand is that becoming Christian does not prevent them from retaining their cultural identity. The Indian Christian has every right to be proud of his heritage and culture. Much of culture is outside the realm of sin and moral judgment, and is perfectly legitimate to be practiced. The Lausanne Covenant states it well:

---

[20] Hiebert, *Anthropological Insights for Missionaries*, pp. 97-98.
[21] Tippett, *Introduction to Missiology*, p. 152.

Culture must always be tested and judged by Scripture (Mark 7:8, 9, 13). Because man is God's creature, some of his culture is rich in beauty and goodness (Matt. 7:11, Gen. 4:21, 22). Because he is fallen, all of it is tainted with sin and some of it demonic. The gospel does not presuppose the superiority of any culture to another, but evaluates all cultures according to its own criteria of truth and righteousness, and insists on moral absolutes in every culture.[22]

Many Christians believe that because we are one in Christ all our differences should disappear. They quote Gal. 3.28 which says, 'There is neither Jew nor Greek, there is neither slave nor free, there is neither male nor female; for you are all one in Christ Jesus'. However, we need to remind ourselves that Paul was speaking of the spiritual dimension rather than the physical. We are one in the Spirit, but physically we are different because of our cultural backgrounds.

Culture, like language, is a tool for communication and interaction. Missionaries cannot communicate without concerning themselves with culture. Lingenfelter and Mayers write,

> God's plan and purpose for us are that we be perfected in Christ Jesus. That means becoming all things to all men. As we live and interact with the people of another culture, we must adapt to their ways. In addition, as we see sin, we must separate the sinner from the culture. It is not culture which is sinful, but the heart of the individual.[23]

God will use the culture of the people to bring them to Himself. Thom Hopler writes,

> God, in his concern for all people, has allowed truth to infiltrate every culture ... There are many culture groups who have the seeds of truth. They are fully ripe for the harvest. We can join that harvest if we will be compassionate, sensitive and humble. Our task is to discover what truth God has already

---

[22] Hesselgrave, *Communicating Christ Cross-Culturally*, pp. 118-19.
[23] Lingenfelter and Mayers, *Ministering Cross-Culturally*, p. 118.

given to a people, emphasize that, and lay aside cultural differences.[24]

In cross-cultural communication, the goal that every missionary should strive for is biculturalism. This is the ability to work comfortably in two cultures, which is something that not too many missionaries achieve. A bicultural person can have his/her social needs met in either culture. Kelly tells the story of a young missionary couple that left the field in mid-term because the wife did not have any 'Christian' fellowship. They were working in a national church which had a large congregation, including a substantial number of women. What this couple actually meant was that the wife did not have any 'White' Christian fellowship. In order to have her social needs met, they returned home. This couple, in almost two terms, had not achieved bi-culturalism.[25]

The North American Indian Worldview

The word 'worldview' refers to how people understand the world around them. The worldview of a people affects every aspect of their way of life. Hesselgrave writes, 'A worldview is the way people see or perceive the world, the way they know it to be. What people see is in part what is there. It is partly what we are. But these combine to form one reality, one worldview.'[26]

Some areas of life can be looked at as worldview universals. Kraft outlines these universals of worldview:

1. The first of these is classification. All peoples classify the reality they perceive around them according to the categories laid down for them in their worldviews. Whether it's plants or animals, people or things, material objects or social categories, natural or supernatural entities, the visible or the invisible – all

---

[24] Thom Hopler, *A World of Difference* (Downers Grove, IL: InterVarsity Press, 1981), pp. 77-78.

[25] Daniel P. Kelly, *Destroying The Barriers* (Vernon, BC: Laurel Publications, 1982), p. 101.

[26] Hesselgrave, *Communicating Christ Cross-Culturally*, p. 197.

are labelled and put into categories together with other items and entities believed to be similar to them ...

2. A second area that all worldviews treat is that of person/group. The nature of the human universe and both its internal and external relationships needs to be understood in the same way by all the members of a society ... We are taught whether to see people primarily as individuals (as in America) or primarily as groups (as in other societies). We are taught whether people are expected to dominate the physical environment (as in western societies) or to submit to it (as in many nonwestern societies) ... In short, whatever a society deems necessary for its members to know concerning people, their nature, and behaviour is codified in a society's worldview.

3. A third area addressed by every worldview is the matter of causality. The questions being answered under this label are questions of power or cause. What forces are at work in the universe? And what results do they bring about? Are the forces personal, impersonal, or both? The answers provided have names like God, gods, spirits, demons, luck, fate, mana, chance, cause and effect, political and economic structures, the power of persons, and so on ...

4. Time is another worldview universal. All worldviews codify their society's concept of time. Daily, weekly, monthly, yearly, seasonal, and other cyclical entities are conceptualized ... Many peoples, for example, are more event oriented than time oriented. That is, they are more concerned with what happens than with how long it goes on. In the West, we set rather strict time limits on most of our activities ...

5. All worldviews likewise provide people with assumptions concerning space. Whether it's a matter of how to arrange buildings, structure in space within buildings, structure interpersonal standing space, sleeping space, eating space, or how to conceive of and relate to geographical features or the universe as a whole, a people's worldview provides the rules ...

6. People find it necessary to define the relationships between the various components of worldview and culture. Whether it is a matter of enabling people to relate time to space, or classification to causality, or space to persons and other relationships between categories, or a matter of relating one kind of time to another (e.g., seasonal time to calendar time), or individuals to groups, or one cause to another (e.g., God to spirits) within the various categories, a worldview provides the guidelines.[27]

The North American Indian people have a worldview that places them at one with nature. The respect they have for the land and nature is largely influenced by their animistic worldview. They believe that spirits dwell within objects and therefore all things have the equal right to live. Some Indian tribes performed rituals to appease the spirits of the animals they killed. The land has always been sacred to Native people because they depend on it for their livelihood. Ovide Mercredi, former National Chief of the Assembly of First Nations, shares how the First Nations view their relationship to the land. He states that we have a 'responsibility to care for and live in harmony' with the land and all creatures. He writes further, 'We believe that the responsibility to care for this land was given to us by our Creator, the Great Spirit. It is a sacred obligation, which means the First people must care for all of Creation in fulfilling this responsibility.'[28]

Belief in a Supreme Being, better known to them as the Great Spirit, is universal among the Indian tribes. The Great Spirit is the Creator of all living things. Creation and providence have a prominent place in the Indian worldview. The spirit world is very real to Native people. Through their vision quests some Indian people have been successful in making contact with supernatural spirits who become their spirit helpers. These spirit helpers or guardian spirits stay with them for life and can be used for good or evil. Kelly writes, 'At the core of Indian worldview is the concept of the acquisition, or control, or manipulation of power. A funda-

---

[27] Kraft, *Anthropology For Christian Witness*, pp. 63-65.
[28] Mercredi and Turpel, *In the Rapids*, p. 16.

mental belief is that an individual must be able to acquire sufficient supernatural energy to function in a mysterious universe.'[29]

A comparison of values shows that white people tend to be conscious of time whereas Native people are not too concerned about it. Native people operate on 'Indian time' in most of their meetings because they are event-oriented. Lingenfelter and Mayers show the difference between time and event orientations.

Time Orientation

1. Concern for punctuality and amount of time required.
2. Careful allocation of time to achieve the maximum within set limits.
3. Tightly scheduled, goal-directed activities.
4. Rewards offered as incentives for efficient use of time.
5. Emphasis on dates and history.

Event Orientation

1. Concern for details of the event, regardless of time expended.
2. Exhaustive consideration of a problem until resolved.
3. A 'let come what may' outlook not tied to any precise schedule.
4. Stress on completing the event as a reward in itself.
5. Emphasis on present experience rather than on the past or future.[30]

Another difference is that Native people are present-oriented while white people are more future-oriented. Dan Kelly makes the distinction of values this way,

> In Western cultures we regard time quantitatively, as a commodity. We sell it, buy it, borrow it, waste it, kill it, make it up, take it, and if we run afoul of the law, we do it. We are obsessed with time. To the Indian, priority belongs to the significant thing he is doing right now.[31]

---

[29] Kelly, *Destroying The Barriers*, p. 252.
[30] Lingenfelter and Mayers, *Ministering Cross-Culturally*, p. 42.
[31] Kelly, *Destroying The Barriers*, p. 258.

Missionaries need to understand the worldview of the people they are working with. The relationship between language and culture are closely intertwined. To speak the language will greatly help the missionary in acquiring an understanding of worldview. Reed, who was a field missionary in North Thailand and taught missions at Briercrest Schools for many years, writes, 'Understanding the what, the why, and the how of worldview and its importance in understanding the people will aid the missionary in becoming an effective communicator for Jesus Christ in another cultural setting'.[32]

Is there a single Christian worldview? Kraft states his personal position this way, with which I concur:

> We have indicated in several ways that the coming of Christianity is intended to bring about change at the deepest level of a people's cultural assumptions. Helping people to develop those assumptions and the habitual behavior appropriate to them is a major concern of Christian growth.
>
> In spite of this fact, I do not believe there is a single Christian worldview. If there were, Christians would need to have a single approach both to things like moral values and to things like time, space, and categorization. There are those who speak of a Christian worldview (e.g., Sire 1976; Schaeffer 1976). They are not understanding, however, the all-encompassing nature of worldview in the anthropological sense. They are speaking of the influx of Christian assumptions, values, and allegiances into a worldview as if that input constituted the whole worldview. It does not.
>
> Christian Africans, Christian Asians, Christian Europeans, and the multitude of committed Christians from the other societies of the world simply do not see most things the same way, in spite of their commitment to Christ. The question is, should they? My answer is no. There will be certain very important similarities. But most of the differences in the worldview, as in surface-level cultural behavior, remain – unless, of course, in the process of becoming Christian, these

---

[32] Reed, *Preparing Missionaries for Intercultural Communication*, p. 104.

people also change their culture. This latter is not, however, a Christian requirement.

Jesus had a worldview. It consisted of His 'Kingdom perspectives' integrated into His first-century Hebrew worldview. Our task is to follow His example by integrating those same perspectives into our cultural worldview. We are to assume Christian assumptions and live habitually by them, each within his or her own cultural context, just as Jesus did within His context.[33]

Concrete Relational Thinking

One of the characteristics of culture is that it is constantly changing. Native people have been able to retain their cultural identity within the last five hundred years because they have learned to adapt to cultural change. The majority of Natives today speak English because of education, and their lifestyle is quite similar to the white society. But we need to remember that culture is in the mind of the people.

Mary Ellen Turpel, an aboriginal rights advocate and professor of law at Dalhousie University writes,

> First Nations peoples have a central place in this society and that place will not be determined by stereotypes of the vanishing Indian or presumptions that traditional values are tied to a bygone era of teepees and buffalo jumps. First Nations peoples' relations with Canada can and will be articulated in a contemporary context, but this will not mean the eradication of traditional values.[34]

Culture is in the mind of the people and no two races or groups think exactly alike. An understanding of the mind is important in cross-cultural communication. A Cree Indian told this story about a Native leader who was asked to lecture to non-Native students. Before the Native leader arrived in the classroom

---

[33] Kraft, *Anthropology For Christian Witness*, pp. 67-68.
[34] Mercredi and Turpel, *In the Rapids*, p. 10.

the teacher had instructed the students to pay attention to how he would be dressed and everything he did during his presentation. When the Native leader came he wore a suit and tie and he carried a brief case where he kept his notes and written material. The point that the teacher was trying to make to his students was that this Native leader dressed and behaved pretty much like a white person. The Native person who told this story concluded by saying that the Native leader may have dressed and behaved like a white person but the students did not see what was in his mind. He appeared like a white person but he thought like an Indian.

Harold Lindsell explains *mind of a people* this way. 'By the mind of a people is meant their thought patterns, the way they themselves reason and react to life in its multiform relationships. Outward actions may be identical, but the mind behind the thought may differ greatly.'[35]

We have to recognize the fact that people are different. Pentecost writes,

> Culture, language, geography, history, social customs, social structures, and religion all affect thought patterns. Thought patterns are expressed in linguistic patterns which include both verbal and nonverbal expressions. The expressions must be understood in order to appreciate the communication process, and capture the mentality of the individual.[36]

Native people have been designated as concrete relational thinkers. Hesselgrave points out that 'in concrete relational thinking, life and reality are seen pictorially in terms of the active emotional relationships present in a concrete situation'.[37] He goes on to say that 'in verbal communication, the concrete relational thinker tends to express, inform, and persuade by referring to symbols, stories, events, objects, and so forth, rather than to general propositions'.[38]

---

[35] Hesselgrave, *Communicating Christ Cross-Culturally*, p. 294.
[36] Pentecost, *Issues in Missiology*, p. 99.
[37] Hesselgrave, *Communicating Christ Cross-Culturally*, p. 302.
[38] Hesselgrave, *Communicating Christ Cross-Culturally*, p. 325.

Kelly, who has done extensive research on cross-cultural communication, mentions that 'a common error made by the majority of Euro-North Americans who have had contact with Indian people, is to assume that because they speak English, they are able to clearly understand English'.[39] He cautions that we are not talking about the Native people having some sort of inferior mentality. In dealing with Native people who are graphic-functional thinkers, Kelly says that the following should be considered:

a. Reduce the abstractions; concrete illustrations and operational definitions should be the norm.

b. The experiential world of the receptor should be the primary focus when considering the code, content and treatment of a message.

c. Scriptural stories should be prepared that relate to the real life situation of the Indian person. These will stimulate meaning and maintain interest. The story should convey one scriptural principle.

d. Single point messages should be developed and should be heavily illustrated by the use of graphics, i.e. film strips, overheads, blackboards. Illustrations must be drawn from life situations.

e. There is no substitute for contact. To enter the experiential world of the Indian, the source must have substantial involvement in the lifeway of the receptor in order to establish common ground.[40]

In missions it is generally accepted that the thought pattern of white people tends to be linear and abstract. However, the thought pattern of Native people is said to be circular and to need a real-life application to deal with the intangible. Pentecost explains how the circular thought pattern operates. He writes,

> The American Indian pattern of storytelling is very similar to the Oriental. He will begin telling a story, and make certain

---

[39] Kelly, *Destroying the Barriers*, p. 128.
[40] Kelly, *Destroying the Barriers*, pp. 146-47.

references to his point, then return to his narration repeating his story with embellishment and more application, until finally he comes to the point and conclusion.[41]

Hesselgrave shares a case in point concerning a correspondence course for Christian pastors in central and southern Africa that met with little response. He writes,

> Some concluded that the pastors lacked the motivation to undertake individual study and that the project should be abandoned. Wiser heads, however, were encouraged to restudy the course materials (which had been prepared mainly by Western missionaries in English and then simply translated into various tribal tongues and distributed). Careful analysis – this time with more Native assistance – indicated that the materials were too abstract and theoretical to engage and hold the attention of the pastors. The courses were revised and a number of appropriate drawings included. This time the response was nothing short of overwhelming.[42]

As a Native person myself, I agree with the concept that Native people are concrete relational thinkers. Missionaries must understand the mind of the Native people if they want to be effective in evangelism. Effective communicators among Native people will see the importance of storytelling. Hesselgrave writes, 'Concretizing is, in fact, the very essence of storytelling, and the Bible – especially the Old Testament – is basically a story, and stories within a story!'[43]

Concluding remarks

Contextualization is a cross-cultural communication principle that translates the gospel in a way that can be easily understood and relevant within the cultural context of the people. Contextualization of the gospel message is evident in the New Testament and

---

[41] Pentecost, *Issues in Missiology*, p. 96.
[42] Hesselgrave, *Communicating Christ Cross-Culturally*, pp. 326-27.
[43] Hesselgrave, *Communicating Christ Cross-Culturally*, p. 332.

it helps indigenous churches to grow. Knowing the culture of the people is a prerequisite of contextualization.

Because Indian people think in graphic and pictorial images, it is important to use storytelling and ample illustrations when communicating the gospel to them. Concrete relational thinking has to do with the cognitive process of Indian people. It shows that culture is in the mind of the people. Contextualization, language, culture, worldview, and concrete relational thinking are all essential elements in cross-cultural communication.

Indian people today know the importance of keeping their cultural identity. They want to preserve their language, culture, and worldview. These three elements are valuable tools in cross-cultural communication. Learning the language is difficult for many missionaries but it is not an impossible goal to strive for. Every missionary should aim to be bicultural and in order to do that he/she must know the language, culture, and worldview of the people.

8

STRATEGY FOR EVANGELISM IN NATIVE MISSIONS

The Need for Strategy

Whatever we do in God's work, it is important to have a plan or strategy. The purpose of a strategy is basically to give us an overall sense of direction along with some accountability. Dayton and Fraser mention that they visited missionaries who seem to be in the business of doing, rather than getting things done. They appear not to have any strategy as to why they are there and what God intends to do because they are there. When asked for their goals and purposes, they give answers which sound fine, such as 'to bring the Word to this people.' Dayton and Fraser concluded that 'they have noble sentiments but time and time again we found that these sentiments were not supported by well-thought-through ideas as to *how* this was to be accomplished or *when* it was to be accomplished'.[1]

The administration of every mission organization recognizes the value of developing a strategy statement because it helps to plan and manage things in an orderly way. As Dayton and Fraser point out, a strategy statement is a plan for the evangelization of a given area. It defines the activity to be done, the area in which it is to be accomplished, and the methods to be employed. Beyond that, it defines the

---

[1] Edward R. Dayton and David A. Fraser, *Planning Strategies for World Evangelization* (Grand Rapids, MI: Eerdmans, 1980), p. 20.

lines of authority and the relationships between the field conference and the home board. The statement ought to be in the hands of every board member, the director of missionaries, every missionary, and every potential recruit for the particular field.[2]

When I was the Executive Director for the Native Evangelical Fellowship of Canada, I prepared a Pastoral Handbook and General Information of NEFC which our office made available to the member churches, workers, and the mission organizations.[3] The contents of the handbook included the general information of NEFC concerning its beginning, purpose of existence, goals and objectives, various ministries, philosophy of finances, the indigenous church, NEFC as denomination, steps to organizing a local church, and the benefits for a Native church joining NEFC. The handbook also included the Letters Patent Incorporating, NEFC By-laws, organizational chart, job descriptions for the workers and field representatives, articles of faith and doctrine, and a sample of a church constitution by one of the NEFC churches. We also included a pastoral manual, and a directory of the NEFC churches and the mission agencies. The main reason why I produced the handbook was to provide information that would be helpful to the members in regard to the overall direction of the organization. I believe that information is a key part of promoting a strategy.

Defining Evangelism

The word 'evangelism' or 'evangelization' originates from the Greek word *euangelion*. Dayton and Fraser point out that there are four forms of the basic word: two verbs meaning 'to proclaim good news', and two nouns, one meaning 'evangelist' and the other meaning the 'good news' brought by the evangelist.[4] In the New Testament *euangelion* is usually translated 'gospel',

The primary task of the Church is to evangelize, which means to spread the good news that Jesus Christ died for our sins and was raised from the dead according to the Scriptures. The gospel of Jesus Christ offers the forgiveness of sins and the gift of eternal life to all

---

[2] Dayton and Fraser, *Planning Strategies for World Evangelization*, p. 21.
[3] See the Appendix for an excerpt from the Handbook.
[4] Dayton and Fraser, *Planning Strategies for World Evangelization*, pp. 70-71.

who repent and believe. A simple definition of evangelism that most Christians would accept is this: 'To evangelize is to communicate the gospel in such a way that men and women have a valid opportunity to accept Jesus Christ as Lord and Savior and become responsible members of his Church'.[5]

There are numerous definitions which express the various aspects of evangelism. Dayton and Fraser observed that they all are responding to the Bible and its various statements and portraits of evangelization as seen in the early church. They point out that our problem is to be *biblically responsible* and yet at the same time find a definition of evangelism that can be used *within a strategy perspective*.[6] Toward a constructive understanding of evangelism Bosch writes,

> In awareness of the essentially preliminary nature of our evangelistic ministry, yet at the same time conscious of the inescapable necessity to be involved in this ministry, we may, then, summarize evangelism as that dimension and activity of the church's mission which, by word and deed and in the light of particular conditions and a particular context, offers every person and community, everywhere, a valid opportunity to be directly challenged to a radical reorientation of their lives, a reorientation which involves such things as deliverance from slavery to the world and its powers; embracing Christ as Savior and Lord; becoming a living member of his community, the church; being enlisted into his service of reconciliation, peace, and justice on earth; and being committed to God's purpose of placing all things under the rule of Christ.[7]

The strategy of missions in evangelism is to establish indigenous churches. They recognize that the local church is the best medium for evangelism. Bosch makes a good point that *evangelism is only possible when the community that evangelizes – the church – is a radiant manifestation of the Christian faith and exhibits an attractive lifestyle*. He adds that if the church is to impart to the world a message of hope and love, of faith, justice and peace, something of this should become visible, audible, and tangible in the church itself. The witness of the life of the believing community prepares the way of the gospel.[8]

---

[5] Dayton and Fraser, *Planning Strategies for World Evangelization*, p. 80.
[6] Dayton and Fraser, *Planning Strategies for World Evangelization*, p. 80.
[7] Bosch, *Transforming Mission*, p. 420.
[8] Bosch, *Transforming Mission*, p. 414.

Several years ago, I heard Leighton Ford speak in Toronto at a Vision 2000 banquet hosted by the Evangelical Fellowship of Canada (EFC). During his message, he did a quick survey on evangelism. He simply asked the people to raise their hands if they accepted the Lord through the ministry of television or radio. Not too many hands went up. Then he asked for a show of hands for anyone who accepted the Lord through the means of gospel literature. Only a few hands went up. Finally he asked how many people accepted the Lord through the personal witness of an individual person. The vast majority of the people raised their hands. I thought he proved his point well to show the importance of personal evangelism.

The Strategy of Indian Missions

Planting indigenous churches has proved to be an effective evangelistic methodology in Indian work. It is reassuring to know that this was the strategy that the Apostle Paul used in his missionary outreach. The Inter-Mission Cooperative Outreach (IMCO) mission agencies understand that evangelism is not complete until the converts are incorporated into a local church. Brock says that it is thoughtless and nonbiblical to lead people to faith in Christ and leave them to develop on their own.[9] Establishing indigenous churches and in the process making disciples is right on track in fulfilling the Great Commission: 'Therefore go and make disciples of all nations, baptizing them in the name of the Father and of the Son and of the Holy Spirit, and teaching them to obey everything I have commanded you' (Mt. 28.19-20 NIV).

According to Lindsell, when the indigenous principles are applied the relationship between missionary and nationals will be wholesome and brotherly. New fields of service will open more quickly for the missionary who has become not the nurse of a sickly child but the father of a mature and responsible adult who has grown normally and naturally from babyhood to adulthood in a framework of the New Testament pattern which is definitive. Lindsell goes on to say that whatever have been the errors of the past and however long it takes to correct these errors on fields already occupied, the new approach to the problem of world evangelization will best be served by

---

[9] Brock, *Indigenous Church Planting*, p. 32.

the use of the indigenous methods of the New Testament and particularly of the Apostle Paul.[10]

The primary purpose of NEFC's existence as a Native Church is to promote the gospel message in all lawful ways and to bring lost souls to a saving knowledge of Jesus Christ. NEFC believes that the best medium for evangelism is the local church. Therefore, it is committed to helping establish strong indigenous churches in Canada. The NEFC yearns to participate in sharing the good news of the Gospel in every reserve, village, town, and city across the Dominion of Canada.[11] NEFC as a National Native Church incorporates the local churches which are the principal means of evangelism.

God has used the indigenous principles to give some direction in Native ministries. The principles are only a tool to help in evangelism and they can be ineffective without the power of the Holy Spirit behind them. We need to teach the indigenous principles, but it is more important to teach the Spirit-filled life to all our missionaries and Native leaders.

As a whole the National Native Church in Canada is very much involved in evangelism. Native Christians today are taking more responsibility and initiative to reach their own people with the gospel. As Indian Christians travel to nearby reserves and communities they are sharing their faith with other Indian people.

In the summer, tent meetings are a popular means of evangelism in many Native communities. In some Indian reserves the local church will organize a tent meeting that will usually last for about a week. The church brings in different preachers and gospel singers, usually Native, and always a number of people are converted. Some of these tent meetings draw a large crowd and it is not uncommon to have as many as one thousand Native people in attendance for a service. Through their gifts and offerings the Native Christians themselves take care of all the expenses for the tent meeting.

Television is also used in evangelism by Native Christians today. In Canada there are a few Native gospel television programs. In some Indian reserves they have satellite television and the Christians will use this means of communication to share the gospel in their

---

[10] Lindsell, *Missionary Principles and Practice*, pp. 312-13.
[11] Joseph Jolly (ed.), *Pastoral Handbook and General Information of NEFC* (Brandon, MB: self-published material, 1993), p. 2.

community. In Garden Hill Reserve, Manitoba, the NEFC church there had a regular time every Sunday for their gospel program. Whenever I was there on a Sunday, I would preach on their program.

During the year the local churches have various evangelistic programs and ministries through their church. Some of the Native churches have annual events such as family camps, conferences, evangelistic meetings, and music festivals. Some of the Native churches that are close together will work together in planning large family camps and area conferences. Other evangelistic activities in the local church would include retreats, seminars, drama, radio broadcast, and gospel literature distribution.

When I was working with NEFC, we would distribute videotapes of the NEFC Conference and the Native Pastors and Christian Workers Retreat. These videotapes contained the messages, teaching material, special music, and various testimonies by Indian Christians. We used the television crew of *Tribal Trails* who always gave us quality videotapes after they edited the material. There was a good response to these videotapes, and by selling them at exact cost we pretty well broke even. The Native Christians played these videotapes in their homes for their friends and family members. The videotapes were a good tool for evangelism. We also distributed cassette tapes of messages and music recorded at the conference. There was also a good response to the cassette tapes, and we distributed literally hundreds all across Canada. The cassette distribution ministry is still popular today because people like to listen to tapes in their cars.

Training Native Leaders

The development of Christian leadership has always been emphasized in Indian missions. One effective way some of the mission agencies have developed Native leadership is through the Indian Bible schools which they established and operated. Over the years quite a number of Native Christians have graduated from an Indian Bible school and some of them are in full-time ministry today. It needs to be mentioned too that there have been a number of Native Christians graduated from non-Native Bible schools.

Inter-Mission Cooperative Outreach (IMCO) is a group of mission agencies that work together in reaching Native North American

Indian people for Christ. In their strategy of developing Native leadership these mission agencies encouraged the idea of theological training by extension. They sponsored the Bible Education by Extension (BEE) as a means of extending the Indian Bible School campus. BEE offered accredited courses through one of the Indian Bible schools and made this program available to anyone who wanted Bible school training but could not live on campus during the year.

The local church is doing its part to produce its own leaders. The Native pastors and the church elders see the need to develop leaders without having to depend too much on workers from outside the church. An effective way the local church develops leaders is through the pastor's preaching, teaching, and counseling. As the Native Christians mature spiritually under their pastor's leadership, they will take on more responsibilities in the church. The Indian pastor who is concerned about developing leadership will share the pulpit ministry with developing leaders in the church.

Mission/Church Relationships

In Native ministries I have often heard missionaries say that the goal in missions is to build the National Native Church and not the mission itself. The idea of this strategy is to give an opportunity for the nationals to take a greater responsibility in reaching their own people with the gospel. Some of the mission agencies have no difficulty accepting this idea and are serious in building the National Native Church in Canada. We just have to wait and see whether all the missions are willing to be a servant to the National Native Church leadership which is largely the result of their ministry.

I believe that we still need mission agencies and that they should continue recruiting missionaries for Indian work. As a Native Christian, my desire is to see the mission agencies and the National Native Church working together in mutual respect and harmony because there is still so much evangelistic work and discipleship teaching that needs to be done.

Fuller's Four Stages of Development in Mission/Church Relations express my view of Native ministries on a national level.

Stage I: Pioneer

Requires the gift of leadership along with other gifts. No believers – the missionary must lead and do much of the work himself.

Stage II: Parent

Requires the gift of teaching. The young church has a growing child's relationship to the mission. But the 'parent' must avoid 'paternalism'.

Stage III: Partner

Requires change from parent-child relation to adult-adult relation. Difficult for both to change but essential to the church's becoming a mature 'adult'.

Stage IV: Participant

A fully mature church assumes leadership. As long as the mission remains it should use its gifts to strengthen the church to meet the original objectives of Matt. 28:19-20. Meanwhile the mission should be involved in Stage I elsewhere.[12]

In his notes Fuller points out that the attitudes developed in each stage affect the succeeding stage. I agree with him that a missionary whose strong leadership gift made Stage I possible, needs to know how to change roles to that of a counselor in Stage IV or may need to move to another area where pioneering ability can be used. I appreciate his comment that the main goal of mission and church should be the same if both are doing God's will.[13]

In my opinion, the National Native Church in Canada is now a mature adult and is at Stage IV. It is important for the IMCO mission agencies to consider this in their working relationship with NEFC. We should look forward to the day when Indian ministries is under the leadership of the National Native Church. The truly indigenous church we have been promoting cannot exist at Stage I or Stage II but must move on to the interdependent relationship of Stage III and Stage IV.

---

[12] W. Harold Fuller, *Mission-Church Dynamics* (Pasadena, CA: William Carey Library, 1980), Appendix G.

[13] Fuller, *Mission-Church Dynamics*, Appendix G.

The transition of authority by SIM to the Evangelical Churches of West Africa (ECWA) proves that this is not an impossible goal to strive for. Fuller writes,

> As the churches grew and Nigerians were trained for the departments, SIM turned over the departments to ECWA. Now all the work in Nigeria comes under ECWA's leadership. Nigerians can understand this – one organization has responsibility for the work. They are also glad to see that this does not mean SIM has left the work. The mission is still there to work with ECWA, even though it is no longer in charge. ECWA has assumed responsibility, and SIM is working with ECWA to help develop her gifts so ECWA can fulfill the Great Commission.[14]

In an article on 'Mission-to-Mission Relationships', Hay writes that ECWA is now a mature church, a denomination in Nigeria, with more than 2200 congregations. She continually assesses her own goals to determine how those fulfill the divine commission. Only in this way will ECWA be able to maintain validity as a mature church.[15]

I have used NEFC as a model for the Native National Church because it is fully autonomous and officially recognized as a church denominational body through its national charter. IMCO missionaries encourage the Native churches they release to affiliate with the NEFC, which is a full participating member of IMCO. Besides NEFC, there are other National Native Church organizations which are under denominational affiliation.

As Executive Director of NEFC, I was directly involved in Mission/Church relationships. One thing I noticed was that the desire to work together for the glory of God was evident on both sides. However, Church/mission conflicts sometimes arose. I felt that the majority of the conflicts were related to a misunderstanding of cross-cultural communications and the different views on philosophies of ministry regarding the indigenous methods. As an attempt to ensure cooperative working relations with the IMCO mission agencies I made the following recommendations:

---

[14] Fuller, *Mission-Church Dynamics*, Appendix H.
[15] Ian M. Hay, 'Mission-to-Mission Relationships', in James H. Kraakevik and Dotsey Welliver (eds.), *Partners in the Gospel* (Wheaton, IL: Billy Graham Centre, n.d.), p. 95.

1. Dialogue between a mission and the National Native Church needs to be encouraged to ensure unity and cooperative working relationships. One of the ways to do this is to have joint meetings now and then between the NEFC Board of Directors and the mission leaders.

2. A mission needs to consult Native leaders and seek their input for any major projects and programs that concern Native outreach ministries. Likewise, the Native leaders need to inform the mission and seek their advice on any major changes or decisions that could affect their working relationships. Inter-dependency between the National Native Church and the mission should be encouraged.

3. Missions should take more interest in the annual NEFC Conference. Missionaries should feel they are welcome to attend the conference with their Indian converts. The conference is one of the best ways to encourage Native believers and at the same time promote NEFC to the Native Christians. Back in the 1980s we used to have large conferences with as many as 600 people in attendance. It was encouraging to see a good number of missionaries come with members from their fellowship group.

4. Missionaries need to be informed of IMCO's support for NEFC as the National Native Church. This would eliminate any misunderstandings that may exist between the missionaries and NEFC in their goal to see the growth of the National Native Church. We are often reminded to build the National Native Church and not the mission. If our vision is the same in building the National Native Church, and we see that happening, then we have every reason to give thanks and praise the Lord.

5. Missionaries and church leaders should speak carefully about each other even in being constructive. Any negative comments can discourage Native fellowship groups and individual Native Christians from joining NEFC. Harold Fuller, former Deputy General Director of Sudan Interior Mission (SIM), says that the most important thing is not the organizational structure but the attitude of the parties to one another. He points out that the most

ideal structure can be ineffective if there is lack of mutual respect, trust, and cooperation.[16]

6. The indigenous principles need to be taught to Native students in Bible school and to the Native churches. These mission principles also need to be taught to missionaries. A proper understanding of these principles would resolve some of the conflicts that exist in Mission/Church relationships.

7. NEFC often has insufficient funds to do adequate field work and to undertake projects. Both missions and churches should be considerate in helping out in areas where they can.

Today, I would add that the Native National Church needs to be more inclusive. I have often wondered what would need to be done to bring all the Native churches together into one body. In one of our NEFC/IMCO business meetings it was suggested by the Mission Directors that if NEFC is to function as a National Church it should incorporate other groups including denominational churches, even white churches with an Indian ministry. NEFC could function like IFMA. Small denominational groups could benefit and gain credibility. There could be greater influence without control.

The original goal of IMCO was that NEFC would be the National Native Church. As more members were added, IMCO took a different structure as the central focus of all the missions working with Canadian Natives. Not all of these promoted NEFC as the national church. Ideally, as shown in the following diagram, Native churches of all denominations would become members of the National Native Fellowship, NEFC. This would be the Partner and Participant relationship of Stages III and IV described above.

Finally, I would recommend that since contextualization is important to evangelism, it needs to be explained and taught to the Native Christians and missionaries. Authentic evangelism is always contextual. In Chapters Five and Six I explain what contextualization means and how it relates to evangelism.

---

[16] Fuller, *Mission-Church Dynamics*, p. 42.

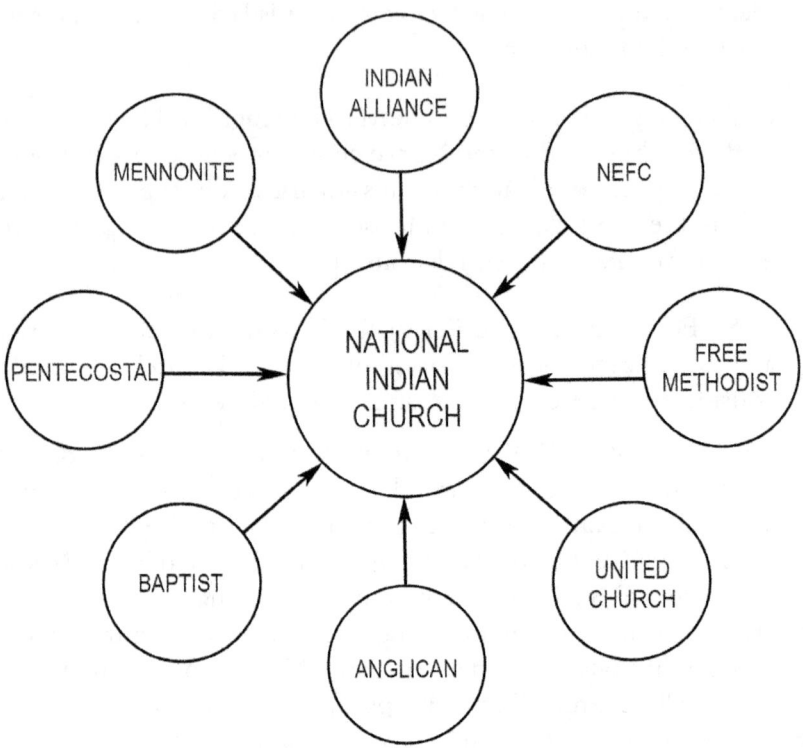

The Church Planter

The church planter may be a missionary, an evangelist, a pastor, or a layman. It is encouraging to see that quite a number of churches have been started by Native Christians. Without a missionary to help them in their area or community these men have taken on the responsibility of pastoring the church while at the same time working full-time in a secular job. In the future we hope to see more of this happening as the Native Christians reach out to their own people.

Church planting requires energy, time, and hard work. It can be stressful work trying to meet the needs of the people. It is also an exciting ministry to be in because there is no greater joy than seeing people come to know the Lord and develop in their Christian walk.

Missionaries should be sure of God's calling because church planting cross-culturally is not something that every Christian can do. There are missionaries today struggling in their ministry because they are not able to minister effectively in a cross-cultural setting. Their love for the Indian people is sincere and they have a genuine burden for their souls, but they find it difficult to communicate and relate to them.

Wagner points out that some well-meaning Christians have actually gone to the mission field and failed because they were not missionaries to start with. Wagner believes that not every Christian has the missionary gift. His definition of the missionary gift is the special ability that God gives to certain members of the body of Christ to minister whatever other spiritual gifts they have in a second culture. It is a specific gift of cross-cultural ministry.[17]

What kind of person should the church planter be? In outlining the qualifications of a church planter, Hodges points out that God sometimes passes by the most likely person, who from a human viewpoint would be most qualified to do the work, and uses unlikely instruments. With no intention of eliminating anyone from the work, Hodges lists the *natural* qualifications of what would normally be expected of a church planter. He writes,

> The church planter should be socially and educationally acceptable to the people he seeks to reach ... Then, because the very nature of church planting requires that the church planter deal with new people, he should have an outgoing personality, be able to meet new people easily, and engage in conversation about spiritual things with all classes of people ... The church planter must be sincerely interested in people and have a deep concern for their personal problems ... Such characteristics as ability in public speaking, an attractive personality, and an exemplary family life will place the minister in a better position to win his hearers to Christ.[18]

As to *spiritual* qualifications, Hodges says, the church planter must be first of all a man or woman of God. They will be filled with the Spirit of God and motivated by a deep and abiding compassion for the lost. The church planter will be a person of prayer and vision. They will be highly motivated, and will persevere in spite of

---

[17] Fuller, *Mission-Church Dynamics*, p. 65.
[18] Melvin L. Hodges, *A Guide to Church Planting* (Chicago: Moody Press, 1973), pp. 28-29.

discouraging setbacks. Their vision is backed up by a solid faith that God has sent them to do this work and will see them through.[19]

My personal thoughts on the qualifications of a church planter would include, first of all, that it is essential for a missionary to know that God has called them to work with Indian people. They should have a one track mind, and that is to reach the Indian people with the gospel.

The missionary should know what his or her spiritual gift is. There are missionaries in the field today whose spiritual gift does not relate well to the task of church planting. For example, a person who has the gift of mercy would probably not fit well in a church planting ministry.

The missionary should have a good background of theological training because, when the church is still young, the missionary is expected to preach, teach, and counsel people. Bible training is a great asset to have in the ministry.

Before going into the field, the missionary should understand cross-cultural communications and what biculturalism means. It is imperative for them to know the missiological concepts of indigenization and contextualization. They need to understand the culture and worldview of the Indian people.

The missionary should be willing to make some personal sacrifices for the sake of establishing an indigenous church. The Indian people are smart enough to know how sincere the missionary is. For example, some missionaries have a Bible study group with the Indian people during the week but they also attend a white church. My personal opinion is that if a missionary is applying the principles of biculturalism then it should not really be a problem for their social and spiritual needs to be met in the Indian church.

Some missionaries still hold to the old traditional approach of missions, without realizing this has hindered their ministry. They need to take a refresher course in missions which will help them to have a contemporary approach in church planting.

---

[19] Hodges, *A Guide to Church Planting*, pp. 29-31.

Essentials in Church Planting

Brock reiterates what so many have said before that an *absolute dependence upon the Lord is an indispensable essential in indigenous church planting.* He says no strategy of planting churches is adequate without divine assistance. Human wisdom or persuasiveness is of value in church planting only as God is in full control.[20]

In church planting the preaching of the gospel message is of prime importance. The message must always be Christ-centered and Bible-based. The local church is established as a result of the message preached. Brock writes that *the gospel seed is another essential in indigenous church planting.* Paul said, 'I have complete confidence in the gospel: it is God's power to save all who believe, first the Jews and also the Gentiles' (Rom. 1.16 TEV).[21]

The missionary is also essential in church planting. Brock writes that *the sower is the third essential in church planting.* The role of the sower or planter is seen in Rom. 10.14-15:

> But how can they call to him for help if they have not believed? And how can they believe if they have not heard the message? And how can they hear if the message is not proclaimed? And how can the message be proclaimed if the messengers are not sent out? As the Scripture says, 'How wonderful is the coming of messengers who bring good news!' (TEV)[22]

Finally, Brock points out that *the fourth essential in church planting is the soil.* He says that church planting is best done in fertile soil. People who are responsive to the gospel provide a more favorable condition for church planting and church growth than those who are not responsive.[23]

In cross-cultural communication the church planter should make every effort for the message to be understood and relevant to the hearers. Because Native people are said to be concrete relational thinkers, it is important to use illustrations and stories when preaching to a Native audience. Speaking the language of the people is a big plus in the communication process. As Kraft points out, a receptor

---

[20] Brock, *Indigenous Church Planting*, pp. 21-22.
[21] Brock, *Indigenous Church Planting*, p. 23.
[22] Brock, *Indigenous Church Planting*, p. 26.
[23] Brock, *Indigenous Church Planting*, p. 27.

oriented communicator will make every effort to meet their receptors where they are. They will choose topics that relate directly to the felt needs of the receptors; they will choose methods of presentation that are appealing to them; and they will use language that is maximally intelligible to them.[24]

In starting an Indian church it is important to concentrate on the adults, because Indian people are family oriented. There is a need for children's ministries later, but in the initial stages of church planting the missionary should try to zero in on the whole family in the evangelistic outreach.

In church planting it is essential for the missionary to confirm in their mind that there is a need to have an Indian church. It will help them to know some of these reasons given by Indian Christians to support the need for an Indian church.

> 1. The reason we need an Indian church is simply because of cultural differences (Herman Williams).

> 2. The gospel message may be more acceptable if presented within the context of an ethnic congregation that is related to the community by race or language (Wilbert Robertson).

> 3. Young Christians tend to grow better among their own kind … It is not racism, but wisdom in reaching people for Christ (Bill Jackson).[25]

The Lord is building His Native Church today even though we make mistakes through our human weaknesses. We still need to continue developing strategies and do all we can to make our ministry effective for the glory of God. Most of all, we need to be sensitive to God's Word and to the Holy Spirit who indwells every believer.

---

[24] Kraft, *Communicating the Gospel God's Way*, p. 7.
[25] George McPeek (ed.), 'The Council Speaks', *Indian Life Magazine* 3 (November/December 1981), p. 12.

9

CONCLUSIONS

Missionaries who are planning to do a church planting ministry with Native people must realize that, like other cultures in the world, the Indian culture is constantly changing. The lifestyle of Indian people has changed considerably since their first encounter with the European explorers and settlers. Native people have never lost their culture and identity because they have learned how to adapt and make cultural changes necessary to suit their contemporary lifestyle. The elders and leaders today recognize the importance of keeping and preserving cultural practices and traditional beliefs for the sake of their children and future generations. It is important for missionaries to apply cross-cultural communication principles in their work with Native people.

The history of Indian missions reveals that during the period 1840-1890 there was a great spiritual awakening among the Native people. There were thousands of Native people who committed themselves to faith in Jesus Christ. However, the revival movement that was so evident eventually lost its momentum and died. One of the reasons was that the denominational missions failed to establish indigenous churches.

Once again there is a spiritual awakening among Native people in Canada which most likely started sometime during the 1950s. Tom Francis became a Christian in 1951 and I remember him saying that in the early years of his ministry he was not able to name even ten Christian leaders who were Indians. Today there are scores of Indian leaders who are serving the Lord either in full-time ministry or by being active and involved in church leadership.

I agree with Dan Kelly that this is probably the most productive era in the history of the missionary movement among North American Indian people. According to Kelly there are three main reasons for this. He writes,

> Politically, socially, economically, and religiously, the Indian people are striving for some form of self-determination. Political pressure groups have been formed in virtually every section of the country. Pan-tribal friendship centers have been established in most municipalities. An increasing number of young Indian people have entered post-secondary educational institutions and are finding employment in the business sector or becoming entrepreneurs themselves. There has been, as well, a young resurgence of interest in traditional belief systems and rituals. This atmosphere of change is the first major force.
>
> A second element is the missionary force which has been mobilized and is ready to take advantage of this climate or change. Not only has there been a noticeable rise in the number of applicants, but the quality of their missions training is improving ... It appears that with improved pre-candidate and missionary development programs the success rate is rising significantly.
>
> The third force which may, in fact, form the catalyst necessary to give meaning to the former two, is the mass of missiological research that has been done especially in the last two decades. In every mission field in the world, missionaries are gathering and compiling volumes of data regarding methodologies, and growth and decline patterns.[1]

The National Native Church is no longer a dream but is a reality. There are hundreds of Native fellowship groups and indigenous churches scattered all across Canada. There are not many Indian reserves in Canada where the gospel has not been presented. In the propagation of the gospel, the Indian Christians are

---

[1] Kelly, *Destroying the Barriers*, pp. 1-2.

doing their part, but we also need to mention that there are several hundred missionaries with the various mission agencies who are active in the mission field across Canada and the territories. Each year there are more Indian people who trust Jesus Christ as their Lord and Saviour – Christ is in the business of building His Native Church.

The big picture in Indian missions is the National Native Church. As the indigenous National Native Church grows spiritually, it will take on more leadership and a greater responsibility in reaching its own people with the gospel of Jesus Christ. The continuing growth of the National Native Church is dependent on recruiting more Native workers and white missionaries to do evangelism and discipleship training. On the one hand, it is wonderful to hear that thousands of Native people have put their faith in Jesus Christ; but on the other hand, the vast majority of Native people are still lost in sin.

As I noted, I have no problem accepting the strategies and theories concerning the missiological concepts of indigenization and contextualization. I recognize they are valuable tools in evangelism. Their primary purpose is to help missionaries present the gospel more effectively in a way that is relevant to the Native people within their cultural context. The indigenous methods and strategies are essential in Native ministries, but they are ineffective without the power of the Holy Spirit. To be able to work together cooperatively in furthering the kingdom of God, we need to teach and live the Spirit-filled life. Only in this way can Christ have the freedom to build His Native Church.

APPENDIX

An Excerpt from the *Pastoral Handbook and General Information of NEFC*, compiled and edited by Joseph Jolly (1993)

THE BEGINNING OF NEFC

The birth of the Native Evangelical Fellowship of Canada, Inc (NEFC), came about as a result of missionary endeavor to the aboriginal peoples of Canada. As Indian men and women were won to Christ they were given Bible School training and encouraged to take leadership in the local churches that were established. As the Native Christians grew in their faith, they soon saw the spiritual need among their own people. They saw this need not only in one reserve but across the Dominion of Canada.

According to the writings of NEFC's Founder, Tom Francis, the formation of the Native Evangelical Church, as NEFC was known then, came about in this order of events. Tom noticed that one of the early missions working in northern Canada among the Natives was experiencing some difficulty in the proclamation of the gospel due to cultural barriers. They came to the conclusion that if they were going to be used of God to reach the Natives and establish the converts, their whole missionary policy and strategy would have to change. Thus the indigenous method in church planting was introduced, although this was not a new concept in world missions.

NEFC began as Native Christians met together each year from various mission stations. These special meetings were encouraged by the mission and individual missionaries. The Island Lake Bible School in northern Manitoba was used since there were already a number of Native leaders there who were attending the school. It was at one of these meetings that the Native Christians first discussed the possibility of a Native Church to improve the work.

In 1957 the idea of having a loosely knit fellowship of Native Christians across Canada was born. The Lord's leading was truly evident as the Native Christians from remote and distant areas were united in their desire to organize a Native Evangelical Church across Canada. In 1968, By-laws and a Constitution were drawn up for the Native Evangelical Church. In 1969 at the General Conference in Winnipeg, Manitoba, the name was changed to the Native Evangelical Fellowship. That same year the NEF under its new name applied for a Charter from the Canadian Federal Government.

On April 1, 1971, the Native Evangelical Fellowship received its Letters Patent Incorporating from the Consumer and Corporate Affairs of Canada. The Native Evangelical Fellowship of Canada, Inc (NEFC), under its new corporate name would now be officially recognized as a non-profit religious charitable organization. Through its National Charter, the NEFC as a Native Church is able to carry out its operations throughout Canada and elsewhere.

The Purpose of NEFC's Existence

Even though the ministry of NEFC has been around for over thirty years, there are still many Native Christians who do not really know the purpose of its existence. This may be one of the main reasons why NEFC does not yet have the full support from its membership churches. There is still a great need to teach the churches and individual member the goals and objectives of NEFC's overall ministry. The administration of NEFC would like to see the membership churches take more responsibility and full ownership regarding the affairs and operations of NEFC.

The primary purpose of NEFC's existence as a Native Church is to promote the gospel message in all lawful ways and to bring lost souls to a saving knowledge of Jesus Christ. NEFC believes that the best medium for evangelism is the local church, and therefore it is committed to helping establish strong indigenous churches in Canada. The NEFC yearns to participate in sharing the good news of the gospel message in every reserve, village, town, and major city across the Dominion of Canada.

NEFC's Goals and Objectives

The NEFC is a Native Church but it also functions as a mission sending agency. As a Native mission, NEFC is able to promote missions and recruit Native missionaries. For many years now the NEFC has been working co-operatively with other Indian missions and is a member with Inter-Missions Cooperative Outreach (IMCO). NEFC sees the need and benefit of maintaining cooperative working relationships with other Native missions that are striving toward similar goals.

NEFC's goal as a mission-sending agency is to recruit Native missionaries who will work among their own people in a church planting ministry. As Native Christians we are grateful for the white missionaries who came and shared the gospel with us, but now we must take a greater responsibility in sharing the gospel with our own people. In missions one of the important characteristics of an indigenous church is to be self-reproducing. The white missions working with Native people still have a very important role to play in Native ministries because the Native Church is still quite young and there is so much work that needs to be done. One area in which the Native Church and the IMCO missions can work together is promoting fellowship and spiritual growth among the Native believers.

The NEFC is not a segregated organization. The NEFC realizes that the gospel is for all people but its chief focus is to reach out and minister to the Native people. The NEFC was raised up to meet the spiritual needs of the Native people and it also plays a major role in encouraging the Indian Christians to be active in their witness for Christ.

Ministries of NEFC

Evangelism
During the year, all of the NEFC churches do their share of evangelistic outreach through the various programs and ministries in their church. A number of these church ministries are now annual events such as family camps, conferences, evangelistic services, and music festivals. It is encouraging to know that some of the Native churches who are near each other, are working together to plan large family camps and area conferences. Generally the speakers and musicians at these special meetings are Native pastors and evangelists.

NEFC General Conference
The annual NEFC General Conference at Caronport, Saskatchewan, always draws many Native Christians from both Canada and the United States. The NEFC Conference provides an ideal setting for Native Christians from many different tribes to have fellowship with one another. The many testimonies, special music groups, and the preaching of the Word of God are always a blessing to everyone who comes.

Native Pastors & Christian Workers Retreat
The Native pastors and Christian workers have enjoyed these annual retreats in Banff, Alberta, because the topics are especially geared for those in the ministry. The opportunity to fellowship and get to know other Native Christian leaders is also another strong motivation to attend these meetings. Like the NEFC Conference the retreat pays for itself through each person covering his own transportation, meals and accommodation expenses. For some of the Native pastors and Christian workers who have a limited income this can be too costly. This is why the NEFC administration raises money for the retreat each year so that it can help those who need some assistance.

Distribution of Gospel Literature
Over the years NEFC has printed and distributed thousands of gospel tracts and other literature for the Native people. At one time NEFC printed a song book which was so well received that

it had to be reprinted three times. This song book is no longer available through our office but it is still being used in many Native congregations today. If the funds become available to expand NEFC's literature ministry in the near future we might reprint the NEFC song book again.

The NEFC News is published quarterly and is sent out to all the NEFC members and individual supporters who are on NEFC's mailing list. The NEFC News is a powerful tool in informing the churches and individual members of NEFC's activities and ministry during the year. In the future NEFC wants to continue to establish and maintain a strong publishing arm for Native gospel literature.

Video and Cassette Ministry

For a couple of years now, the NEFC has been making and distributing video tapes of the NEFC Conference, and teaching material from the Native Pastors and Christian Workers Retreat. There has been a fairly good response to this new venture even though we have not really publicized it. We are very grateful to the crew from the *Tribal Trails* television ministry who have been using their cameras and equipment to tape all the sessions. To distribute the video tapes does not cost NEFC very much, because for each tape our office sells, we get our money back. This is a worthwhile ministry that needs to be developed in the future. It is also an effective way to promote NEFC's ministry to the Native people.

The NEFC also distributes cassette tapes of music and recorded Bible messages. The cassette ministry is still quite popular and reaches its peak at every NEFC Conference. Cassette recordings of both the messages and the special music at the Conference are always in demand. Over the years NEFC has distributed literally thousands of cassette tapes all across Canada.

NEFC's Philosophy of Finances

The NEFC encourages all of its membership churches to be self-supporting through the believers' tithes and offerings. As the Lord blesses each Christian, all are to give unto the Lord (Mal. 3.10; Lk.

6.38; 2 Corinthians 8-9). God's work will go forward because of the believers' faithfulness in giving.

Each local church is to take the initiative and be responsible to purchase or to rent facilities for their fellowship. The financing for the land or church building should come from the local Christians and people in the community. The Native believers should not rely on or report to mission boards for finances.

The local churches will also be responsible for the financial support of their pastor. If the church is not able to give their pastor a full salary right away, the pastor should get a part-time job to supplement his/her income. The NEFC missionaries who are working full-time in the ministry are required to raise their own personal support.

Reaching any people with the gospel costs money. The NEFC relies upon Almighty God, first, to direct His people to support its ministry. Any work that is beginning depends on outside resources, and the NEFC is no different in this respect. The NEFC looks to the future when outside support will no longer be solicited, but rather the Native Indian indigenous churches will be fully supporting NEFC.

The Indigenous Church

God's Church is made up of people who have put their faith in the Lord Jesus Christ and have been born again by the Holy Spirit. The members of God's Church come from many different nationalities with each having their own culture. Even though people may be different by the colour of their skin, their language, and their way of life, in God's sight we are all brothers and sisters in the Lord and therefore belong to the family of God. Because of the love of Christ in our hearts we can love each other, respect each other, and appreciate one another. God has led His Church in each nationality of people to serve Him. The nationals preach His Word and share His love and as a result their own people are won into God's family.

God desires His Church to be present among the Native people of Canada. The Lord in a wonderful way has given birth to

His Church among the Indian people that is independent and indigenous. This Church goes under the name of the Native Evangelical Fellowship of Canada, Inc (Tom Francis).

In Native ministries today, the application of the indigenous church principles is very important. This is understandable if the goal of every Indian mission is to establish indigenous churches. The key point in teaching the indigenous principles is to train Native Christian leaders to reach their own people with the gospel. Missionaries who have been on the field for many years will testify that Indians reaching Indians is the quickest and most effective way to present the gospel to Native people.

The indigenous church when applied to mission work means, 'As a result of missionary effort, a national church has been produced which shares the life of the country in which it is planted and finds within itself, the ability to govern itself, support itself and reproduce itself'. (Melvin L. Hodges)

NEFC as a Denomination

Even though NEFC is a fellowship of Indian churches, in the eyes of the government it is a religious denomination because of its incorporation. The NEFC does not emphasize its identity as a church denomination but would rather be looked on as a fellowship. There is no religious hierarchy in NEFC because NEFC believes in the full autonomy of its membership churches. The NEFC administration can approach a member church only when there is a doctrinal difference or a violation of a by-law which each member church has agreed to follow.

Steps to Organizing a Local Church

There is no set formula in organizing a local church but these suggestions might be helpful for your fellowship.

1. There should be a nucleus of believers who are mature and indoctrinated in spiritual truths.

2. From the fellowship group there should be some kind of government for the Christians to govern their weekly activities

and church business. If the believers are still immature in their spiritual growth, it might be wise to form a Church Committee rather than to appoint a Church Board.

3. Within the Church Committee, officers should be elected for the transaction of church related business.

4. If the fellowship group wants to become a member of NEFC, they can write to the NEFC office to get the information they need. An NEFC representative will make a point to visit the church and explain to the believers NEFC's ministry.

5. If the Native fellowship is still quite young it can apply for associate membership. At a later date it can apply to become a formal member.

6. If a fellowship group wants to join NEFC as a formal member, it usually means that the believers have been meeting together as a church for some time. The NEFC encourages all fellowship groups who apply for formal membership to submit a copy of their church constitution and by-laws. In the long run this will help them to get better organized. The NEFC has sample copies of church constitutions which the fellowship churches can use for a guide.

Note: For a local church to get their registration number for tax purposes, the government requires a copy of their church constitution and by-laws along with their application.

Benefits for a Native Church Joining NEFC

If your fellowship group is thinking of joining NEFC in the near future here are some of the benefits it can receive.

1. You will become part of the many Indian fellowship groups all across Canada who are already members of NEFC.

2. You will have identification and affiliation with a Native Christian organization of your own kind. Instead of being independent and alone you will be in a group that also agrees with your doctrine and love for Jesus Christ.

3. NEFC will help your fellowship group to get established as a local church.

4. NEFC will help your pastor obtain ordination and issue a licence to solemnize marriages.

5. NEFC will help in church discipline for exceptional cases that may be difficult for the local church to handle.

BIBLIOGRAPHY

Books

Allen, Roland, *Missionary Methods: St. Paul's or Ours?* (Grand Rapids, MI: Eerdmans, 1962).

Bosch, David J., *Transforming Mission: Paradigm Shifts in Theology of Mission* (Maryknoll, NY: Orbis Books, 1991).

Brock, Charles, *The Principles and Practice of Indigenous Church Planting* (Nashville, TN: Broadman Press, 1981).

Cassidy, Frank (ed.), *Indigenous Self-determination* (Lantzville, BC: Oolichan Books, 1991).

Champagne, Duane, *Native America: Portraits of the Peoples* (Detroit, MI: Visible Ink Press, 1994).

Dayton, Edward R. and David A. Fraser, *Planning Strategies for World Evangelization* (Grand Rapids, MI: Eerdmans, 1980).

Frideres, James S., *Native Peoples in Canada: Contemporary Conflicts* (Scarborough, ON: Prentice Hall Canada, 3rd edn, 1988).

Friesen, John W., *Rediscovering the First Nations of Canada* (Calgary: Detselig Enterprises, 1997).

Fuller, W. Harold, *Mission-Church Dynamics* (Pasadena, CA: William Carey Library, 1980).

Grant, John Webster, *Moon of Wintertime* (Toronto: University of Toronto Press, 1984).

Hay, Ian M., 'Mission-to-Mission Relationships', in James H. Kraakevik and Dotsey Welliver (eds.), *Partners in the Gospel* (Wheaton, IL: Billy Graham Centre, n.d), pp. 91-107.

Hedican, Edward J., *Applied Anthropology in Canada: Understanding Indigenous Issues* (Toronto: University of Toronto Press, 1997).

Hesselgrave, David J., *Communicating Christ Cross-Culturally* (Grand Rapids, MI: Zondervan, 2nd edn, 1991).

—*Planting Churches Cross-Culturally* (Grand Rapids, MI: Baker Book House, 1980).

Hesselgrave, David J. and Edward Rommen, *Contextualization – Meanings, Methods, and Models* (Grand Rapids, MI: Baker Book House, 1989).

Hiebert, Paul G., *Anthropological Insights for Missionaries* (Grand Rapids, MI: Baker Book House, 1985).
—*Anthropological Reflections on Missiological Issues* (Grand Rapids, MI: Baker Book House, 1994).
Hodges, Melvin L., *A Guide to Church Planting* (Chicago: Moody Press, 1973).
—*The Indigenous Church* (Springfield, MO: Gospel Publishing House, 1976).
Hopler, Thom, *A World of Difference* (Downers Grove, IL: InterVarsity Press, 1981).
Jenness, Diamond, *Indians of Canada* (Toronto: University of Toronto Press, 7th edn, 1977).
Jacobs, Donald R., 'Contextualization in Missions', in James M. Phillips and Robert T. Coote (eds.), *Toward the Twenty-first Century in Christian Mission* (Grand Rapids, MI: Eerdmans, 1993).
Jolly, Joseph (ed.), *Pastoral Handbook and General Information of NEFC*. (Brandon, MB: self-published, 1993).
Kane, J. Herbert, *Understanding Christian Missions* (Grand Rapids, MI: Baker Book House, 4th edn, 1986).
Kelly, Daniel P., *Destroying the Barriers* (Vernon, BC: Laurel Publications, 1982).
—*Indigenous Church Principles* (Vernon, BC: Laurel Publications, 1977).
Kraft, Charles H., *Communicating the Gospel God's Way* (Pasadena, CA: William Carey Library, 1983).
—*Anthropology for Christian Witness* (Maryknoll, NY: Orbis Books, 1995).
—*Christianity in Culture* (Maryknoll, NY: Orbis Books, 1995).
Kraft, Charles H. and Tom N. Wisley (ed.), *Readings in Dynamic Indigeneity* (Pasadena, CA: William Carey Library, 1979).
Lindsell, Harold, *Missionary Principles and Practice* (Westwood, NJ: Fleming H. Revell Company, 1955).
Lingenfelter, Sherwood G. and Marvin K. Mayers, *Ministering Cross-Culturally* (Grand Rapids, MI: Baker Book House, 1986.
Luzbetak, Louis J., *The Church and Cultures* (Maryknoll, NY: Orbis Books, 1996).
Mandelbaum, David G., *The Plains Cree* (Winnipeg: Hignell Printing Limited, 1979).
Masters, D.C., 'Canada', in J.D. Douglas (ed.), *The New International Dictionary of the Christian Church* (Grand Rapids, MI: Zondervan, 1978, pp. 185-87.
McGavran, Donald A., *Understanding Church Growth* (Grand Rapids, MI: Eerdmans, 1970).

McGavran, Donald A. and Winfield C. Arn, *Ten Steps for Church Growth* (San Francisco, CA: Harper & Row Publishers, 1977).

McLean, John, *The Indians of Canada* (Toronto: Coles Publishing Company, 1970).

McMillan, Allan D., *Native Peoples and Cultures of Canada* (Vancouver, BC: Douglas & McIntyre, 1988).

Mercredi, Ovide and Mary Ellen Turpel, *In the Rapids* (Toronto: Penguin Books Canada, 1993).

Morrison, R. Bruce and C. Roderick Wilson, *Native Peoples: The Canadian Experience* (Toronto: McClelland & Stewart, 2nd edn, 1995).

Morse, Bradford W (ed.), *Indigenous Peoples and the Law* (Ottawa, ON: Carleton University Press, 1989).

Muller, Richard A., *The Study of Theology* (Grand Rapids, MI: Zondervan, 1991).

Pentecost, Edward C., *Issues in Missiology* (Grand Rapids, MI: Baker Book House, 1982).

Ponting, J. Rick, *Arduous Journey: Canadian Indians and Decolonization* (Toronto: McClelland & Stewart, 1991).

Purich, Donald, *Our Land* (Toronto: James Lorimer & Company, Publishers, 1986).

Reed, Lyman E., *Preparing Missionaries for Intercultural Communication: A Bicultural Approach* (Pasadena, CA: William Carey Library, 1985).

Smith, Craig Stephen, *Whiteman's Gospel* (Winnipeg: Indian Life Books, 1977).

Sogaard, Viggo, 'Dimensions of Approach to Contextual Communication', in Dean S. Gilliland (ed.), *The Word Among Us* (Dallas, TX: Word Publishing, 1989), pp. 160-81.

Soltau, Stanley T., *Missions at the Crossroads* (Wheaton, IL: VanKempen Press, 1954).

Stanley, Charles, *The Wonderful Spirit Filled Life* (Nashville, TN: Thomas Nelson Publishers, 1992).

Stott, John R.W. and Robert Coote (ed.), *Down to Earth* (Grand Rapids, MI: Eerdmans, 1980).

Thiessen, Henry C., *Lectures in Systematic Theology* (Grand Rapids, MI: Eerdmans, 1976).

Tippet, Allan, *Introduction To Missiology* (Pasadena, CA: William Carey Library, 1987).

Twiss, Richard, *Culture, Christ, and the Kingdom Seminar* (Vancouver, WA: Wiconi International, 1996).

Van Rheenen, Gailyn, *Missions: Biblical Foundations & Contemporary Strategies* (Grand Rapids, MI: Zondervan, 1996).

Verkuyl, J., *Contemporary Missiology: An Introduction* (Grand Rapids, MI: Eerdmans, 1978).

Wagner, C. Peter, *On the Crest of The Wave* (Ventura, CA: Regal Books, 1984).

—*Spiritual Power and Church Growth* (Altamonte Springs, FL: Strang Communication Company, 1986).

Walls, Andrew F., *The Missionary Movement in Christian History: Studies in the Transmission of the Faith* (Maryknoll, NY: Orbis Books, 1996).

Walsh, Gerald, *Indians in Transition* (Toronto: McClelland & Stewart, 1971).

Wilson, Robert, 'Ryerson, Adolphus Egerton', in J.D. Douglas (ed.), *The New International Dictionary of the Christian Church* (Grand Rapids, MI: Zondervan, 1978), p. 868.

Young, Egerton Ryerson, *The Apostle of the North: James Evans* (London: Marshall Brothers, 1899).

—*By Canoe and Dog Train* (Prince Albert, SK: Northern Canada Evangelical Mission Press, 1991).

Zeleny, Robert O (exec. ed.), *The Indian Book* (Chicago: World Book - Childcraft International, 1980).

Zunkel, C. Wayne, *Church Growth under Fire* (Scottsdale, PA: Herald Press, 1987).

Periodicals

Cowan, Len, 'An Indigenous Church for Indigenous People'. *Faith Today* 9 (July/August 1991), p. 23.

Elford, L.W., 'Freeing the Slaves of Canada'. *Good News Broadcaster* 37 (October 1979), p. 37.

Goar, Carol, 'Why Ottawa's Plan Has Natives Angry', *The Toronto Star* (28 September 1991), p. D5.

McPeek, George (ed.), 'The Council Speaks'. *Indian Life Magazine* 3 (November/December 1981), p. 12.

Other Bibliographical Sources

Assembly of First Nations, 'Description of the Assembly of First Nations' (Ottawa 1999). Accessed from http://www.afn.ca/afndesc.htm, 15 October 1999).

'NCEM: Past & Present' (Unpublished paper in the records of Northern Canada Evangelical Mission).

Francis, Tommy, 'The Formation of the Native Evangelical Church' (Unpublished paper in the records of Native Evangelical Fellowship of Canada).

—Charlie Lee and Jerry Sloan, 'Working with the Indian Church.' Unpublished paper in the records of Native Evangelical Fellowship of Canada).
Jacobs, Adrian, 'Indigenous Christianity the Way It Was Meant to Be' (Belleville, ON: self-published manuscript, 1998).
—'The Meeting of the Two Ways' (Winnipeg: Indian Life Ministries) http://www.indianlife.org/twoways. htm, 8 February 2000.
Quequish, Gary, 'Effective Biblical Counselling Among Ojibway Peoples' (MA thesis, Briercrest Biblical Seminary, 1994).
Statistics Canada, *1996 Census: Indigenous Data.* 13 January, 1998).

Index of Biblical References

Genesis
4.21, 22   121
9.1   17
11   17
11.9   17

Isaiah
40.30-31   108

Malachi
3.10   157

Matthew
7.11   121
28.19-20   136, 140

Mark
7.8, 9, 13   121

Luke
6.38   157-58

John
1.1-4   113

Acts
9.20-22   112
13.16, 17   112
14.15-17   113
15.19   x
17.2, 3   112
17.22-33   112
17.31-32   113
21.37, 40   117
22.2   117

Romans
1.16   147
3.28-30   113
10.14-15   147

1 Corinthians
9.19-24   94

2 Corinthians
8-9   158

Galatians
1.6-9   113
3.28   121

Ephesians
3.19   113

Index of Authors

Allen, R. 84, 85
Arn, W.C. 76
Bosch, D.J. 38, 135
Brock, C. 114, 116, 136, 147
Cassidy, F. 13
Champagne, D. 8, 9
Church, C. x
Coote, R. 39, 97
Cowan, L. 52, 53, 55, 56, 60
Dayton, E.R. 133, 134, 135
Elford, L.W. 44
Francis, T. 49, 50, 51-56, 75-78
Fraser, D.A. 133-35
Frideres, J.S. 26, 27, 34
Friesen, J.W. 17, 34
Fuller, W.H. 140, 141, 143, 145
Goar, C. 25
Grant, J.W. 29, 30, 32, 33, 42-45
Hay, I.M. 141
Hedican, E.J. 5, 6, 8, 11, 23
Hesselgrave, D.J. 101, 111, 112, 113, 114, 115, 117, 118, 121, 122, 128, 130
Hiebert, P.G. 89, 91, 92, 94, 97, 99, 100, 101, 105, 106, 107, 120
Hodges, M.L. 54, 58, 61, 71, 72, 79, 145, 146
Hopler, T. 121, 122
Jenness, D. 6, 7
Jacobs, A. 98, 106, 107
Jacobs, D.R. 39, 74, 108
Jolly, J. 137
Kane, J.H. 68
Kelly, D.P. 33, 42, 76, 117, 122, 125, 129, 150
Kraft, C.H. 68, 97, 114, 117, 122, 124, 126, 127, 146, 148
Lee, C. 77, 78
Lindsell, H. 2, 3, 50, 51, 66, 80, 128, 136-137
Lingenfelter, S.G. 118, 119, 121, 125
Luzbetak, L.J. 92

Mandelbaum, D.G. 21
Masters, D.C. 30, 31
Mayers, M.K. 118, 119, 121, 125
McGavran, D.A. 75, 76, 84, 113
McLean, J. 20, 21
McMillan, A.D. 10, 11, 12, 16
McPeek, G. 148
Mercredi, O. 12, 17, 19, 26, 124, 127
Morse, B.W. 6, 9
Muller, R.A. 93
Pentecost, E.C. 3, 18, 97, 98, 118, 128-30
Phillips, J.M. 39
Ponting, J.R. 35, 36, 37
Purich, D. 14, 23
Quequish, G. 24, 99
Reed, L.E. 111, 116, 117, 126
Rommen, E. 101
Sloan, J. 77, 78
Smith, C.S. 81, 104
Sogaard, V. 92
Soltau, S.T. 4
Stanley, C. 3, 84
Stott, J.R.W. 97
Thiessen, H.C. 91
Tippet, A. 70, 71, 80, 120
Turpel, M.E. 12, 17, 19, 26, 124, 127
Twiss, R. 36, 91, 93, 95, 100, 102, 103, 104, 106, 108
Van Rheenen, G. 36, 58, 59, 82, 83
Verkuyl, J. 37, 38, 68, 74, 82
Wagner, C.P. 76, 98, 145
Walls, A.F. 39
Walsh, G. 7
Wilson, C.R. 19
Wilson, R.B. 19, 40
Wisley, T.N. 68
Young, E.R. 40, 41, 42, 43
Zeleny, R.O. 15
Zunkel, C.W. 84

www.ingramcontent.com/pod-product-compliance
Lightning Source LLC
LaVergne TN
LVHW020930090426
835512LV00020B/3288